A New Edition of a Free Enquiry Into the Miraculous Powers Which Are Supposed to Have Subsisted in the Christian Church, From the Earliest Ages Through Several Successive Centuries

MEMORIAL OF THE PROTESTANT MARTYRS: RIDLEY, LATIMER, AND CRANMER; ADJOINING THE NORTH END OF MAGDALEN PARISH CHURCH YARD, OXFORD.

A NEW EDITION

OF

A FREE INQUIRY

INTO

THE MIRACULOUS POWERS

WHICH ARE SUPPOSED TO HAVE SUBSISTED IN

THE CHRISTIAN CHURCH,

FROM THE EARLIEST AGES THROUGH SEVERAL SUCCESSIVE CENTURIES, UPON THE AUTHORITY OF

The primitive Fathers.

BY

CONYERS MIDDLETON, D.D. CAMBRIDGE,

Author of the celebrated Life of Cicero, of A MOST IMPORTANT LETTER FROM ROME, *and of other searching investigations, who published this Work in* 1749, *and died* 1750.

LONDON:

J. AND W. BOONE, 29, NEW BOND STREET,

AND ALL BOOKSELLERS.

OCTOBER 10th, 1844.

Price 1*s. or* 9*s. per doz.*]

Extract from the Works of the excellent Chillingworth, who was born 1602 *and died* 1644, *æt.* 42.

"The Bible, I say, the Bible, is the religion of Protestants. I, for my part, after a long, and (as I believe and hope) impartial search after the true way to eternal happiness, do profess plainly that I cannot find any rest for the sole of my foot but upon this rock only. I see plainly, and with my own eyes, that there are Popes against Popes, and Councils against Councils; some Fathers against other Fathers; the same Fathers against themselves; a consent of Fathers of one age against a consent of Fathers of another age; traditive interpretations of Scripture are pretended, but there are few or none to be found. No tradition but that of Scripture can derive itself from the fountain, but may be plainly proved either to have been brought in in such an age of Christ, or that in such an age it was not in. In a word, there is no sufficient certainty but of Scripture, for any considering man to build upon. This, therefore, and this only, I have reason to believe. This I will profess, according to this I will live; and for this, if there be occasion, I will not only willingly, but gladly lose my life, though I should be sorry that Christians should take it from me."

This quotation is taken from some Letters against Calvinism, Romanism, and the Athanasian Creed (page 37*): to which is added a Letter to the Bishop of London, denying the exercise of any Miraculous Powers in the Administration of the Sacraments. Third Edition. Boone, Bond Street. Price 6d. each, or 3s. per doz.*

AN INQUIRY
INTO THE SUPPOSED MIRACULOUS POWERS
OF
THE PRIMITIVE FATHERS.

I NOW procede, according to my promise, to a more precise and accurate discussion of the argument of the *Introductory Discourse*, and to open all the particular proofs, which induced me finally to embrace it, with that freedom and impartiality which becomes every ingenuous and disinterested inquirer after truth: and, that I may lay the whole question before the reader in the clearest light, I propose to observe the following method.

I. To draw out, in their proper order, all the principal testimonies, which relate to the miraculous gifts of the church, as they are found in the writings of the fathers, from the earliest ages, after the days of the Apostles. Whence we shall see, at one view, the whole evidence, by which they have hitherto been supported.

II. To throw together all, which those fathers also have delivered, concerning the condition of the persons who are said to have been indued with those

---

In the opinion of the editor, the times seem to call for this edition of Dr. Middleton's work. The Introductory Discourse and the many notes of this able and learned writer have been omitted in order to offer a comprehensive view of the subject adapted more especially to readers in general.

gifts, and to have wrought the miracles, to which they appeal.

III. To illustrate the particular characters and opinions of the fathers who attest those miracles, so as to inable us to determine with more exactness what degree of credit may be due to their testimony.

IV. To review all the several kinds of miracles which are pretended to have been wrought, and to observe from the nature of each how far the credibility of them may reasonably be suspected.

V. To refute some of the most plausible objections which have hitherto been made by my antagonists, or which the prejudices and prepossessions of many pious Christians may be apt to suggest to the general turn of my argument.

I. In collecting all the facts and testimonies, which relate to the present argument, from the earliest antiquity, after the days of the Apostles, our first thoughts are carried of course to the *Apostolic* Fathers, that is, to those, who had lived and conversed with the Apostles, and who, by their special appointment, were ordained to succeed them in the government of the Church. For as there are several of this character, whose writings still remain to us, *St. Barnabas, St. Clemens, St. Ignatius, St. Polycarp, St. Hermas*, so it is natural to expect, that, in these valued remains, the history of the miraculous gifts, which are so much celebrated by the writers of the New Testament, should be carried on still in the same manner by these their immediate successors, through the next generation. For if any such gifts had been actually subsisting in their days, it is highly probable, that men of their eminent zeal and piety, who had seen the wonderful effects of them, under the management of the Apostles, and must themselves have possessed a large share of them, would have made some appeal or reference to them, in their circular epistles to the Churches, as their predecessors had done, for the honor of the Gospel, and the credit of their own ministry. But instead of this, it is remarkable, that there is not the least claim or pretension, in all their several pieces, to any of those extraordinary gifts, which are the subject of this inquiry; nor to any standing power of working miracles, as residing still among them, for the conversion of the heathen world. The whole purpose of their writings is, to illustrate the excellence and purity of the Christian doctrine; and the whole power of their ministry seems to have lain in the innocent and amiable character of their lives, and in the pious, charitable, and fervent strain of their pastoral exhortations.

They speak indeed in general, of certain *spiritual gifts*, as abounding among the Christians of that age: yet these cannot reasonably be interpreted to mean anything more than the *ordinary gifts and graces* of the Gospel, *faith, hope, and charity; the love of God and of man;* which they all recommend in the warmest terms, and appear to have possessed in the highest degree. *Archbishop Wake* however, who has translated their works into *English*, says, that *in all probability, they were indued with the extraordinary gifts of the Holy Spirit, and that there are sufficient indications of it in their writings:* "which he endeavours to confirm, not by any facts or express testimonies, drawn from themselves, but by inferences onely or conjectures, grounded on a supposed frequency of those indowments in that age, and the communication of them, as he says, to much lesser and worser men; on the sanctity of their lives, and the greatness of the stations, to which they were called by the Apostles; and on the accounts of them, transmitted to us by their Successors: from all which he concludes, that they were not onely instructed by persons inspired, but were themselves also in some measure inspired too, or indued with the extraordinary gifts of the Holy Ghost." But whatever gifts of this sort there may be supposed to have possessed, it is certain at least, as the same translator of their works takes occasion to inculcate, that their endowments were *far inferior, both in their kind and degree,* to those of their predecessors, the Apostles.

But the learned *Mr. Dodwell,* a writer of a more sanguin complexion, peremptorily declares, from the mere title or address of *St. Ignatius's* Epistle to the Church of *Smyrna,* that miracles subsisted in great abundance in those days, because that Church is there stiled, *blessed with every good gift and wanting in no good gift.* Yet these words, as they are explained by the context, manifestly signify nothing more than the ordinary gifts of the Gospel, *faith and charity,* for the whole passage runs thus: *To the Church of God the Father, and of the beloved Jesus Christ, which God hath mercifully blessed with every good gift, being filled with faith and charity so as to be wanting in no good gift.* In another Epistle likewise of *St. Ignatius* to the *Romans*, written on his journey towards *Rome*, whither he was going to suffer martyrdom, there are these words: "I am willing to die for God, unless you hinder me. I beseech you that you show not an unseasonable goodwill towards me; suffer me to be food for the wild beasts, by whom I shall attain unto God; for I am the wheat of God and shall be ground by the teeth of the wild beasts, that I may be found the pure bread of Christ," &c. From which words the same learned person again infers, *that the prayers of the primitive Christians had the power to disable the wild beasts from assaulting the martyrs, who were exposed to them in the amphitheatres.* Yet the passage itself has not the least reference to prayers, or to anything miraculous, but to the ordinary endeavours and intercession of the Christian brethren at *Rome*, who offered to use their interest to preserve him from that cruel death which he was then going to suffer; to which sense it is expressly restrained in the relation of his martyrdom, written by those who accompanied him in this very journey, and were present at his death, by whom we are told: "That the brethren who came out to meet him on his approach to that city, and were zealous for his safety, *undertook to appease the people*, so that when he came to be exposed to the wild beasts in the amphitheatre *they should not desire his destruction*; but the Saint over-ruled, *and commanded them to be quiet.*" And to the same sense also Dr. *Cave* has interpreted it in his *Life of this Saint.* "The Christians at *Rome*," says he, "came out to meet and entertain him; and when some of them did but intimate that possibly the people might be taken off from desiring his death, he expressed a pious indignation, intreating them to cast no rubs in his way that might hinder him, now he was hastening to his crown."

And in truth, all the other expressions of these fathers, which are commonly understood to signify the extraordinary gifts of the Holy Ghost, may be interpreted more rationally and more agreeably to the general turn of their writings, to denote onely the ordinary graces of the Gospel, faith, and charity; which they constantly extoll, as superior to all other perfections; as *things wonderfull and admirable;* and *the peculiar gifts of God:* nay in some places, they seem even to disclame all gifts of a more extraordinary kind. Thus *Polycarp*, in his Epistle to the *Philippians*, says, "These things, my brethren, I took not the liberty to write to you of myself, concerning righteousness, but you before encouraged me to it. For neither I, nor any other such as I am, can come up to the wisdom of the blessed and renowned *Paul.*" And in the same Epistle he declares, that it was not granted to him, to practise that, which is written in the Scripture; *be angry and sin not, and let not the sun go down upon your wrath.*" St. *Ignatius*, also, in his Epistle to the *Ephesians*, says: "These things I prescribe to you, not as if I were somebody extraordinary, for tho' I am bound for his name I am not yet perfect in

Jesus Christ, but now I begin to learn, and speak to you as to fellow disciples. For I ought to have been stirred up by you in faith, in admonition," &c.

This same Saint indeed, in one or two of his Epistles, seems to intimate that the knowledge of certain events had been communicated to him by the Spirit. Thus in his Epistle to the *Philadelphians,* speaking of the earnest exhortations which he had given them to unity and submission to their *bishops, priests, and deacons,* he says: "Some people suspected that I was acquainted beforehand with the divisions among you; but he is my witness, for whom I am bound, that I did not know it from any human flesh, but the Spirit declared it, speaking thus, *do nothing without your bishop,*" &c. From which Dr. *Wake* takes occasion to infer, *that he was indued with a large portion of the extraordinary gifts of the Holy Ghost:* yet I do not find that any other commentator has ventured to build anything miraculous or supernatural upon it.

It is related likewise of *Polycarp,* in the ancient narrative of his martyrdom, "how in the time of that persecution, in which his life was particularly sought for by the heathen magistrates, he withdrew himself from *Smyrna,* by the advice of his friends, into a little village, where he spent his days and nights in prayer, with a few who accompanied him; and as he was praying, a vision was offered to him, three days before he was taken, in which he saw his pillow on fire: whereupon, turning presently to his companions, he said prophetically, I must certainly be burnt alive." The same narrative calls him also a *prophetic teacher;* and declares, *that every word which he uttered had either been fulfilled, or would be fulfilled.* Whence some later writers have affirmed, that he was indued with a spirit of prophesy, and fortold everything that was to happen to him. But the foresight of his death, and the manner of it, in the time of a cruel persecution, when his person was particularly hunted from village to village, as the principal and destined sacrifice, may reasonably be considered as the effect of common prudence, without recurring to anything miraculous.

Here then we have an interval of about half a century, the earliest and purest of all Christian antiquity after the days of the Apostles, in which we find not the least reference to any standing power of working miracles, as exerted openly in the church for the conviction of unbelievers; but, on the contrary, the strongest reason to presume that the extraordinary gifts of the apostolic age were by this time actually withdrawn; and the Gospel left to make it's way by it's own strength, and the authority of those credentials and original miracles with which Christ had furnished it, as an effectual security of its success and triumphs over the powers of the earth. Yet before we take leave of these apostolic fathers it may be proper to observe, for the prevention of unnecessary cavils, that if from the passages referred to above, or from any other which may be found in them, it should appear probable to any that they were favoured on some occasions with *extraordinary illuminations, visions, or divine impressions*, I shall not dispute that point with them, but remind them only that the gifts of that sort were merely personal, granted for their particular comfort, and reaching no farther than to themselves, and do not therefore in any manner affect or relate to the question now before us.

But if the apostolic writers have left us in the dark with regard to our present argument, their successors it must be owned, as far as their authority reaches, have cleared it from all obscurity by their strong, explicit, and repeated attestations of many extraordinary gifts and miraculous powers which were constantly and publicly exerted in the Christian Church through each succeeding age.

Justin Martyr, who is supposed to have written his first Apology within fifty years after the days of the Apostles, says, "There are prophetical gifts among us at this day, and both men and women indued with extraordinary powers by the Spirit of God. And he frequently appeals, to what every one might see with his own eyes, in every part of the world, and particularly in *Rome*, in the case of persons possessed with devils; who were cured and set free, and the devils themselves baffled and driven away by the Christians, adjuring or exorcising them in the name of *Jesus*, when all other exorcists and enchanters had tried in vain to help them."

Ireneus, who was contemporary with *Justin*, but wrote somewhat later, and lived much longer, affirms, "That all who were truly disciples of *Jesus*, receiving grace from him, wrought miracles in his name, for the good of mankind, according to the gift, which each man had received: some cast out devils, so that those from whom they were ejected, often turned believers, and continued in the Church; others had the knowledge of future events, visions, and prophetical sayings: others healed the sick by the imposition of hands: that even the dead had been raised, and lived afterwards many years among them: that it was impossible to reckon up all the mighty works, which the Church performed every day, to the benefit of nations; neither deceiving, nor making a gain of any, but freely bestowing what it had freely received." And as to the particular miracle of *raising the dead*, he declares it "to have been frequently performed on necessary occasions; when by great fasting, and the joint supplication of the Church of that place, the spirit of the dead person returned into him, and the man was given back to the prayers of the saints." And again, "we hear many, says he, in the Church indued with prophetic gifts; speaking with all kind of tongues; laying open the secrets of men for the public good; and expounding the mysteries of God.

Theophilus, Bishop of *Antioch*, who lived in the same age with *Irenæus*, speaking of the *evil and seducing spirits*, which used to inspire the poets and prophets of the heathen world, says, "the truth of this is manifestly shewn, because those who are possessed by such spirits, are sometimes exorcised even at this day by us, in the name of the true God; when these seducing spirits confess themselves to be the same dæmons, who had before inspired the heathen poets.

Tertullian, who florished towards the end of the second, and died in the beginning of the third century, challenges the heathen magistrates, "to call before their tribunals, any person possessed with a *devil*; and if the evil spirit, when exorcised by any Christian whatsoever, did not own himself to be a devil, as truly, as in other places, he would falsely call himself a God, not daring to tell a lie to a Christian, that then they should take the life of that Christian: and what is more manifest, adds he, than this operation; what more convincing than this proof?" In another place "there is a sister," "says he, among us, indued with the gifts of revelations, which she suffers in the Church, during the time of divine service, by an ecstasy in the spirit: she converses with Angels, and sometimes also with the Lord: sees and hears mysteries: and knows the hearts of some, and prescribes medicines to those, who want them."

Minucius Felix, who is supposed to have written in the beginning of the third century, addressing himself to his heathen friend, in his Dialogue, called *Octavius*, says; "the greatest part of you know, what confessions the dæmons make concerning themselves, as oft as they are expelled by us out of the bodies of men, by the torture of our words, and the fire of our speech. *Saturn* himself, and *Serapis*, and *Jupiter*, and the rest of them, whom you worship, constrained by the pain, which they feel, confess what they are; nor in this do they tell us a lie, tho' it be to their own shame, especially when some of your people are present. Believe them therefore to be dæmons, from their own testimony, and true confession. For being adjured by the true and onely God, they unwillingly and wretchedly betray their uneasiness in the bodies of men; and either fly out instantly, or vanish gradually, in proportion as the faith of the patient, or the grace of the agent assists towards the cure."

Origen, who lived at the same time with *Minucius*, tho' something younger, declares; "that there remained still among the Christians of his days, the manifest indications of that Holy Spirit, which was seen in the shape of a dove. For they drive away devils, says he; perform many cures; foresee things to come; according to the will of the divine word: and tho' *Celsus* and the *Jew*, who is introduced by him, will make a jest of what I am going to say, I will say it nevertheless; that many people, as it were against their wills, have been brought over to Christianity, by the Spirit giving a sudden turn to their minds, and offering visions to them either by day or by night; so that instead of hating the word, they became ready even to lay down their lives for it. I have seen many examples of this sort; and should I onely set down such of them as were transacted in my presence, I should expose myself to the loud laughter of the unbelievers, who imagine that we, like the rest whom they suspect of forging such things, are imposing our forgeries also upon them: but God is my witness, that my sole purpose is, to recommend the religion of *Jesus*, not by fictitious tales, but by clear and evident facts."

In another place, he says; "that miracles began

with the preaching of *Jesus*, were multiplied after his ascension, and then again decreased; but that, even in his days, some remains of them continued with a few, whose souls were cleansed by the word, and a life conformable to it." Again; "Some," says he, in proof of a miraculous power received through faith in Christ, "heal the sick, by invoking the name of God over them, and of *Jesus*, with a recital of some story of his life. I myself have seen many so healed in difficult cases; loss of senses, madness, and innumerable other evils, which neither men nor devils could cure." Again, speaking of devils; "We are so far," says he, "from worshipping them, that by prayers and the rehearsal of some passages of the sacred writ, we drive them before us, out of men and places, and also out of beasts; for they sometimes attempt to do mischief also to these." Then as to the method of performing this miracle, "It was not," he says, "by any curious, magical, or inchanting arts, but by prayer alone, and certain plain adjurations or exorcisms, which any simple Christian might perform: for even common and illiterate laymen were generally the actors in this case." In which no man was more eminent than one of his own disciples, *Gregory*, called the *Wonder-worker*, who cast out devils, not only by word of mouth, but even by *a message, or mandatory letter to them*; as the ecclesiastical writers have recorded of him.

Cyprian, the scholar of *Tertullian*, who wrote about the middle of the third century, speaking of *prophetic visions*, which was the peculiar gift of that age, says; "Besides the visions of the night, even boys among us are filled with the Holy Ghost, and in fits of ecstacy, see, hear, and speak things, by which the Lord thinks fit to instruct us." And describing all the various pranks of the devils, "They insinuate themselves," says he, "into the bodies of men, raise terrors in the mind, distortions in the limbs, break the constitution, and bring on diseases;—yet adjured by us in the name of the true God, they presently yield, confess, and are forced to quit the bodies which they possessed. You may see them by our command, and the secret operation of the divine power, lashed with scourges, scorched with fire, tortured by an increase of pains; howling, groaning, begging; confessing whence they came, and whither they go, even in the hearing of their own worshippers: and they either fly out immediately, or vanish gradually, according to the faith of the patient, or the grace of him who works the cure." In another place, treating again on the same miracle, "It is performed," says he, "at this day, so that the devil is lashed and burned and tortured by the exorcists, with human words, but a divine power; and when he promises to go out, and to dismiss the men of God, he often deceives, and by the same lie of obstinacy and fraud, does what *Pharoah* had done before, till he is oppressed by the salutary water of baptism."

Arnobius, who is supposed to have published his book against the Gentiles, in the year of Christ 303, tells us, "that Christ used to appear sometimes in those days to just and holy men, not in vain dreams, but in his pure and simple form: and that the mention of his name put the evil spirits to flight; struck their prophets dumb; deprived the Southsayers of the power of answering; and frustrated the acts of arrogant Magicians; not by the terror or hatred of his name, as the Heathens pretended, but by the efficacy of his superior power."

Lactantius, the disciple of *Arnobius*, who florished and wrote about the same time, speaking of those dæmons or evil spirits, says; "that being adjured by the Christians in the name of God, they retire out of the bodies of men; and being lashed by their words as by scourges, confess themselves to be dæmons; and even tell their names; the same which are adored in the temples; and this even in the presence of their worshippers; yet casting no reproach on religion, but on their own honor, because it is not in their power to lie either to God, in whose name they are adjured, or to the just, by whose voice they are tortured: wherefore after many howlings, they frequently cry out that they are scourged and burned, and are going out instantly."

These are the principal testimonies which assert the miraculous gifts of the Primitive Church, through the three first centuries: which might be supported still by many more of the same kind, and from the same as well as different writers, if it were necessary. But these are sufficient for our purpose: and the warmest admirers of those ages will not scruple, I dare say, to risk the fate of the cause upon the merit of them: for if these cannot command belief, the credit of the miracles in question must sink at once; since Christian antiquity can furnish no other evidence in their favor half so strong and authentic as this.

I shall close this first article with a remark or two, which it seems naturally to suggest. It has already been observed, that the silence of all the Apostolic writers on the subject of these gifts, must dispose us to conclude that in those days they were actually withdrawn. And if this conclusion be thought to have any weight in it, then surely the pretended revival of them, after a cessation of forty or fifty years, and the confident attestation of them made by all the succeding Fathers, cannot fail of infusing a suspicion of some fiction in the case. For if they did really cease for so long an interval, and at a time when the Christian cause seemed to want them the most, as being then deprived of it's first and ablest champions,—the Apostles; we cannot conceive any reason why they should afterwards be revived, when the Church, without any such help, had been gathering more and more strength all that while, by its own natural force. But it is remarkable, that as the Church continued to increase in power and credit, so it's miraculous gifts are said to have increased also in the same proportion: for tho' by an increase of power it certainly stood less in need of true miracles, yet by the same power it became more able to reward, and more like therefore to excite false pretensions to them.

Again, the difference which every one may perceive between the miraculous gifts of the Apostolic days, and these of the following ages, not onely in the nature, but in the manner also of exerting them, will greatly confirm the suspicion just intimated. The Apostles wrought their miracles on special occasions, when they felt themselves prompted to it by a divine impulse; but at other times were destitute of that power; as it is evident from many facts and instances recorded in the New Testament. Agreeably to which, tho' they appeal sometimes, in confirmation of their mission, to the miraculous works which their Master had inabled them to perform; yet we never find them calling out upon the magistrates and people to come and see the mighty wonders which they were ready to exhibit before their eyes, on all occasions, at any warning, and in all places, whenever they thought fit. Whereas this confident and ostentatious manner of proclaming their extraordinary powers, carries with it an air of quackery and imposture, as it was practised by the primitive wonder-workers; who, in the affair especially of casting out devils, challenge all the world to come and see with what a superiority of power they could chastise and drive those evil spirits out of the bodies of men, when no other *Conjurors*, *Inchanters*, or *Exorcists*, either among the Jews or the Gentiles, had been able to eject them.

II. Under this head, I shall briefly lay before the reader all such notices as I have been able to draw from any of the primitive writers, concerning the persons who were indued with these extraordinary gifts, and wrought the several miracles to which they appeal.

Now whenever we think or speak with reverence

of these primitive times, it is with regard always to these very Fathers, whose testimonies I have been collecting; who have left behind them, in their writings, the genuin specimens of their sanctity and abilities. "*Venerable saints, and eminent lights of the best and purest ages*, as *Dr. Waterland calls them, and of admirable indowments, ordinary and extraordinary*." And they were indeed the chief persons and champions of the Christian cause in those days; the Pastors, Bishops, and Martyrs of the Primitive Church. Yet none of these '*Venerable Saints* have any where affirmed, that either they themselves, or the Apostolic Fathers before them, were indued with any power of working miracles, but declare only in general, "that such powers were actually subsisting in their days, and openly exerted in the Church; that they had often seen the wonderful effects of them; and that every body else might see the same whenever they pleased." But as to the persons who wrought them, they leave us strangely in the dark; for instead of specifying their names, conditions, or characters, their general stile is, "such and such works are done among us, or by us; by our people; by a few; by many; by our Exorcists; by ignorant laymen, women, boys, and any simple Christian whatsoever:" but in the particular case of *casting out devils*, *Origen* expressly says, *that it was performed generally by laymen*. Agreeably to which Mr. *Whiston* declares, "that this gift, which he ranks amongst the greatest of miracles, was wholly appropriated by our Saviour to the meaner sort of Christians, with an exclusion even of the clergy; so that, after the days of the Apostles, none of the sacred order ever pretended to it."

But of what condition soever the actors were, it is certain that in the performance of their miracles they were always charged with fraud and imposture by their adversaries. *Lucian* tells us, *that whenever any crafty Juggler, expert in his trade, and who knew how to make a right use of things, went over to the Christians, he was sure to grow rich immediately, by making a prey of their simplicity.* And *Celsus* represents all the Christian wonder-workers as mere vagabonds and common cheats, "who rambled about to play their tricks at fairs and markets; not in the circles of the wiser and better sort, for among such they never ventured to appear; but wherever they observed a set of raw young fellows, slaves, or fools, there they took care to intrude themselves and to display all their arts." *Cæcilius* also calls them *a lurking nation; shunning the light; mute in public; prating in corners.*

The same charge was constantly urged against them by all the other enemies of the Christian Faith, *Julian*, *Porphyry*, &c.; of whom Dr. *Waterland* however has taken occasion to declare, *that they had some regard to truth in what they said, and to public report, and to their own characters.* But as this seems to have been an hasty and inconsiderate concession, made to serve a particular point which he was then urging, that *the ancient infidels were better men than the moderns*, so I shall lay no stress upon it, but observe onely on the whole, that from these short hints and characters of the primitive wonder-workers, as given by both friends and enemies, we may fairly conclude, that the celebrated gifts of those ages were generally engrossed and exercised by private Christians, chiefly of the layety; who used to travel about from city to city, to assist the ordinary Pastors of the Church and Preachers of the Gospel in the conversion of the Pagans, by the extraordinary gifts with which they were supposed to be indued by the Spirit of God, and the miraculous works which they pretended to perform.

And here again we see a dispensation of things ascribed to God, quite different from that which we meet with in the New Testament. For in those days the power of working miracles was committed to none but the Apostles, and to a few of the most eminent of the other disciples, who were particularly commissioned to propagate the Gospel, and preside in the Church of Christ. But upon the pretended revival of the same powers in the following ages, we find the administration of them committed, not to those who were instructed with the government of the Church; not to the successors of the Apostles, to the Bishops, the Martyrs, or the principal champions of the Christian cause; but *to boys, to women, and above all, to private and obscure laymen,* not onely of an inferior, but sometimes also of *a bad character.* But if those venerable Saints and Martyrs were not indued with them when living, they had amends made to them when dead, if we can believe the reports of their successors, by a profusion of them on their bones and reliques: which suggests a farther cause of suspecting the faith and judgement of those early ages. For how can we think it credible, that God should withhold his distinguishing favors from his faithful servants when living, to bestow them on their rotten bones? or employ his extraordinary power to no other use, but to perpetuate a manifest imposture in his Church? since it is to those ancient tales, so gravely attested, of miracles wrought *by the bones of Saints and Martyrs*, that the Church of *Rome* owes all that trade, which she still draws from the same fund and treasure of her wonder-working reliques: and if we can believe such stories, as they are delivered to us by the primitive writers, we cannot condemn a practice which is evidently grounded upon them.

These things, I say, are so strange, as to give just reason to suspect, that there was some original fraud in the case; and that those strolling wonder-workers, by a dexterity of juggling, which art, not Heaven, had taught them, imposed upon the credulity of the pious Fathers, whose strong prejudices and ardent zeal for the interest of Christianity, would dispose them to embrace, without examination, whatever seemed to promote so good a cause. That this was really the case in some instances, is certain and notorious; and that it was so in all, will appear still more probable when we have considered, in the next place, the particular characters of the several Fathers on whose testimony the credit of those wonderful narratives depends.

III. The authority of a writer who affirms any questionable fact, must depend on the character of his veracity and of his judgement. As far as we are assured of the one, so far are we assured that he does not willingly deceive us; and from our good opinion of the other, we persuade ourselves that he was not deceived himself: but in proportion as there is reason to doubt of either, there will always be reason to doubt of the truth of what he delivers. Nay, in many cases, the want of judgement alone has all the same effect as the want of veracity too, towards invalidating the testimony of a witness: especially in cases of an extraordinary or miraculous nature, where the weakness of men is the most liable to be imposed upon; and the more so, as it happens to be joined to the greater piety and simplicity of manners. Since this then is the sole rule of determining the measure of credit, which is due to a witness of any strange and quæstionable facts, I shall apply it to the case before us, and examine what proofs of a sound judgement and strict veracity are to be found in the writings of those Fathers, who attest the miraculous stories which we are now considering.

As to the Apostolic Fathers of whom I have spoken above, since they have contributed but little towards the illustration of the present quæstion, and bear no direct testimony in it, or none at least but what confirms the point which I am defending, there is no reason to enter into the consideration of their particular characters. Their works, as I have said, are translated into *English*, so that every one may judge of them for himself. They appear to have been men of great piety, integrity, and simplicity;

and that is all, I think, which we need to declare of them on this occasion.

Justin Martyr comes next, whose genius will best be illustrated by some specimens of it, extracted from his writings. We have seen above, that among the indowments conferred in an extraordinary manner on the primitive Christians, *the gift of expounding the Holy Scriptures,* or the *mysteries of God,* was reckoned one: and this, as *Justin* frequently affirms, *was granted by the special grace of God to himself.* Let us inquire then what use he made of this divine gift: and if ever he was really inlightened by it, we might surely expect to find the effects of it there, where he is discoursing *on the mystery of the Cross;* which he declares to be the greatest symbol of power and dominion, and explanes in the following manner. "Consider," says he, "all the things in the world, whether they could be administered, or have any communication with each other, without this form of the Cross. The sea could not be passed, unless that trophy called the sail were preserved in the ship: the earth could not be tilled without it: for neither diggers nor artificers could do their work but by instruments of this shape. The form of man differs in nothing else from other animals, but in the erection of his body, and the extension of his arms, and the projection of his nose from the forehead, through which respiration is made, and which shews nothing else but the figure of the cross: in which sense also it is spoken of by the prophet; *Christ the Lord is the breath before our face.*" Upon this passage the very pious and learned Dr. *Grabe* makes the following remark, which I would recommend to all the zealous admirers of these *venerable saints* and *purest ages*: "*that the holy Martyr must not be rashly blamed, for an interpretation so forced and far fetched; because it was the prevailing custom of that age to import into the sacred text senses which did not belong to it.*"

Again: "Hear," says *Justin*, "how Christ, after he was crucified, fulfilled the symbol of the tree of life in Paradise, and of all the other things which were to happen afterwards to the righteous. For *Moses* was sent with a rod to redeem his people: with this rod he divided the sea; brought water out of the rock; and with a piece of wood made the bitter water sweet. *Jacob* also with sticks made his uncle *Laban's* sheep bring forth such lambs as were to be his own gain, &c." And so he goes on, in this way of allusion, to apply all the sticks and pieces of wood in the Old Testament to the Cross of Christ: and pursuing the same argument in another place, where he is describing the fight of the *Israelites* with *Amalek*, he says, "that when the son of *Nun*, called *Jesus*, led the people on to battel, *Moses* employed himself in prayer, with his hands stretched out in the form of a cross; that as long as he continued in that posture, *Amalek* was beaten; but when he remitted any thing of it, his own people suffered: and that all this was owing to the power of the cross: for the people did not conquer because *Moses* prayed, but because while the name of *Jesus* was at the head of the battel, *Moses* was exhibiting the figure of the Cross." It would be endless to run through all the interpretations of the same kind which are to be found in this Father, since his works are but little else than a wretched collection of them; the pure flights of an enthusiastic fancy and heated brain, which no man in his sober senses could mistake for divine revelations. Yet as absurd as they now appear to be, this pious Father insists that they were all suggested to him from Heaven, and appeals to the *Jews* themselves, against whom he was applying them, *whether they thought it possible for him, to acquire so perfect a knowledge of the Holy Scriptures, if he had not received from the author of them, the grace or gift to understand them.* What credit then can be due to this Father, in the report of other people's gifts and inspirations, who was so grossly deceived himself, or willing at least to deceive others, in this confident attestation of his own? Dr. *Cave* tells us, that *Justin was wholly ignorant of the Hebrew tongue,* which was the cause of his childish blunders whenever he meddled with it. "Every one," says he, "who has dipped but ever so little into that tongue, knows, that *Satan* in the *Hebrew* signifies an adversary: but see the ridiculous interpretation of *Justin.* He is called *Satanas,* says the Martyr; a name compounded agreeably to his nature, of *Sata,* which signifies an Apostate, and *Nas,* a serpent," &c. But for a farther illustration of his character, I shall give an instance or two of the doctrines, which he teaches as orthodox and Apostolical, as well as of the facts, which he asserts as certain and unqsestionable.

He declares, that all the Christians, who were in

all points orthodox, embraced and believed the doctrine of the *millennium*: "that all the Saints should be raised in the flesh, and reign with Christ in *Jerusalem*, enlarged and beautified in a wonderful manner for their reception, in the enjoyment of all sensual pleasures, for a thousand years before the general resurrection." Which doctrine he deduces from the testimony of the Prophets and of St. *John* the Apostle, and was followed in it by the Fathers of the second and third centuries: yet the doctrine itself was afterwards exploded, as it well deserved, not onely as absurd and monstrous, but as impious and heretical. St. *Jerom* treats it as a mere fable, or *dream of the* Jews, *and Judaizing Christians*. Yet from the authority of those Fathers who asserted it, and the credit which it had obtained with the generality of Christians, he foresaw, as he tells us, *what a furious storm he should raise against himself by that freedom*. The sure fate of all those, who in any age of the Church, from the earliest times down to the present, have had the virtue and courage to attack any popular error, or reigning superstition.

He asserts another doctrine full as monstrous; "that God having created the world, committed the care of it to Angels, who transgressing their duty, fell in love with women, and begot children on them, whom we call Dæmons; who subdued mankind to their power, partly by magical writings, partly by terrors, and punishments, and partly by the institution of sacrifices, fumes, and libations, of which they began presently to stand in need, after they had enslaved themselves to their lusts and passions," &c. And in another place, "the truth," says he, "shall come out; that evil Dæmons of old debauched women and corrupted boys, and spread terrors among men, who did not examine things by reason, but seized with fear, and not knowing that these Dæmons were evil spirits, called them Gods, and gave every one that name, which they had each taken to themselves. But when *Socrates* by true reason endeavoured to expose their practices, and draw men away from their worship, they, by the help of wicked men, took care to get him put to death, as an Atheist and impious person."

He professes likewise the highest regard for certain spurious books, which were published under the names of the *Sibyl* and *Hystaspis;* which he treats with the same reverence as the Prophetic Scriptures; appeals to them as divine, and says, that "*by the contrivance of Dæmons, it was made a capital crime to read them,* in order to deter men from coming at the knowledge of what was good, and keep them still in subjection to themselves; which yet, adds he, they were not able to effect; for we not onely read them freely without fear, but offer them also, as you see, to your perusal, knowing that they will be found acceptable to all." And it is certain, that from this example and authority of *Justin,* these silly writings were held in the highest veneration by the Fathers and rulers of the Church, thro' all succeding ages.

Clemens of Alexandria supposes them to have been inspired by God, in the same manner as the Prophets of the Old Testament; which he confirms by the authority both of St. *Peter* and of St. *Paul,* whom he cites as appealing to them for a prediction of the life and character of *Jesus.* "For as God," says *Clemens,* "out of his desire to save the *Jews,* gave them Prophets, so raising up Prophets also to the *Greeks,* from their own nation and language, as far as they were capable of receiving that good gift of God, he separated them from the vulgar, as not onely the Preaching of *Peter,* but the Apostle *Paul* also declares; speaking thus, *take the Greek books into your hands, and look into the* Sibyl, *how clearly she speaks of one God, and of the things to come; then take* Hystaspes *also and read, and you will find the Son of God much more clearly and evidently described; and that many Kings shall employ all their forces against Christ, out of their hatred to him, and to all who bear his name.*"

The heathens on the other hand charged the Christians with the forgery of these books, and gave the title of *Sibyllists,* by way of contempt to those who held them to be divine: which charge the Fathers constantly denied and treated as a pure calumny. Yet all the Critics of these days allow the fact to be true, and consider it as one of the pious frauds of those primitive ages. *There is no man,* says Dr. *Cave, who does not see that they were forged for the advancement of the Christian faith.* Some impute the fraud to *Hermas;* some to *Papias;* and others to *Justin* himself. Mr. *Blondel* and Mr. *Dodwell* charge it upon the Heretics, called *Montanists;* but by a gross mistake, as Dr. *Cave* observes, since *Montanus* was not in being till forty years after *the Sibylline books* were known to the world.

Justin affirms also that silly story concerning the *Septuagint version* of the Old Testament. "That it was made by seventy elders sent for that purpose from *Jerusalem* to *Ægypt,* at the request of King *Ptolemy;* whom that King shut up in as many separate cells, and obliged them each to translate the whole Bible apart, and without any communication with each other: yet all their several translations were found to agree verbatim from the beginning to the end, and by that means were demonstrated to be of divine inspiration." And to raise the greater attention to his story, he introduces it by declaring, "that he is not telling us a fable or forged tale, but that he himself had seen at *Alexandria* the remains of those very cells in which the translators had been shut up." But repeating the same story in his Apology, he makes an unhappy blunder, by saying, that *King* Ptolemy's *message, to beg the assistance of those seventy translators, was sent to* Herod, *King of* Jerusalem; whereas *Herod* happened to live about three hundred years later than *Ptolemy.* Dr. *Grabe* endeavours to excuse *Justin* by the help of a forced criticism, which the ingenious editor of *Justin's* Apology with good reason derides; since this pious Father was certainly guilty here of that weakness against which St. *Paul* warned both *Timothy* and *Titus,* of *giving too much heed to profane,* Jewish, *and old women's fables,* and furnishes a pregnant instance how easily his prejudices might impose upon him in all other cases of the like nature.

To these specimens of his want of judgement, I might add several more, from his frequent use of *fabulous and apochryphal books*, forged by the first Christians under the names of the Apostles, and likewise from his false and negligent manner of quoting the genuin Scriptures. Dr. *Grabe* has collected several instances of the first sort, and his learned editor finds frequent occasion to animadvert upon the second.

It will be said perhaps that these instances shew indeed a weakness of judgement, yet do not impeach the veracity of *Justin* as a witness of fact. With regard to which, we must call to mind what is hinted above, that the want of judgement alone may, in some cases, disqualify a man as effectually from being a good witness as if he wanted veracity too. For example, *Justin* expressly affirms, *that he had seen the cells, in which the seventy were shut up to the task of translating the Bible.* Now it is certain that there never were any such cells, nor any such translators; and the best excuse which can be made for him is, that he was imposed upon by some *Jews* or *Christians* of *Alexandria,* who might shew him some old ruins under the name of cells, which his prepossession in favor of the story, owing to his natural credulity and want of judgement, made him take to be really such.

Again, in his Apology, addressed to the Emperor and Senate of *Rome,* he charges them with paying divine honors to the Heretic and Impostor, *Simon,* of *Samaria*, commonly called the *Magician*; and for the truth of his charge, appeals to a Statue, then subsisting in *Rome*, and publicly dedicated to that *Simon* in the Island of the *Tiber*, with this Inscription, SIMONI DEO SANCTO. But it is manifest beyond all reasonable doubt, as some learned men have shewn, that *Justin* was led here into a gross blunder by his usual want of judgement and knowledge of *Roman* affairs, and his pre-conceived belief of certain fabulous stories which passed current about this *Simon* among the first Christians; for the Statue and Inscription, to which he appeals, were not dedicated to his Countryman, *Simon Magus*, of whose Deification there is not the least hint in any *Roman* writer, but to a *Sabine Deity*, of ancient worship in *Rome*, and of similar name, SEMONI SANCO, frequently mentioned by the old Writers; as the Inscription itself, dug up, about two centuries ago, from the ruins of that very place, or little Island, which *Justin* describes, has clearly demonstrated.

Now should we allow these cases to be clear of any fraud or design to deceive, yet they yield so bad a sample of his understanding, as to render his testimony of very little weight in any other relation whatsoever. For if he was deceived in such plain and obvious facts, where a common discernment and moderate knowledge of history would have enabled him to have discovered the truth, how much the more easily would he be caught by a confederacy of subtle and crafty impostors, employing all their arts to amaze and dazzle the senses of the credulous, and to put off their surprizing tricks for the miraculous effects of a divine power?

I cannot dismiss this Father without taking notice of an accusation which he frequently brings against the *Jews, that they had expunged many passages out of the* Greek *Bibles, in which the character and sufferings of* Jesus *were clearly described:* which charge all the learned of these later ages have found to be wholly groundless. Let us see then how he supports it. "They have erased," says he, "out of the book of *Esdras* the following words: *Esdras* said to the people, this passover is our Saviour, and our refuge; and if you will but persuade yourselves, and be convinced in your hearts, that we are to humble him in a sign or figure, and afterwards to put our trust in him, this place shall not be made desolate to all ages, says the Lord of Hosts. But if you do not believe on him, nor attend to his preaching, you shall be as dirt to the nations." The editor of *Justin* remarks here, that this passage is not to be found in any copies either of the *Apochryphal* or *Canonical Esdras;* nor in any other Christian writer, but *Lactantius;* and instead of being expunged by the *Jews, appears to have been forged by the Christians:* where he refers us to the censure of an able critic and protestant divine, *John Croius,* who charges the forgery on *Justin* himself, in the following words: "To propose what I think, freely and candidly, and what all honest and religious judges of these matters will allow to be true; I take this to have been a pious fraud of *Justin,* in which *Lactantius* followed him;

who forged and published this passage for the confirmation of the Christian doctrine, as well as the greatest part of the *Sibylline Oracles*, and the sentences of *Mercurius*."

Again; *Justin* affirms, that in the 90th Psalm it was said, *tell the nations, that the Lord reigned from the tree*: and that the *Jews* had erased the words, *from the tree*. But as there is no footstep of these words, either in the Vulgate or any of the *Greek* or *Hebrew* copies, it is manifest, says the editor, that *they were not expunged by the* Jews, *but added by the* Christians. Lastly, he charges them with *expunging a passage of* Jeremiah, which yet he owns to be retained in some copies of their synagogues: as it actually is in all copies, both *Greek* and *Hebrew*, to this day. Upon which the editor says, *that he absolves the* Jews *again from all fraud, but cannot absolve* Justin *from the utmost negligence and rashness*. So unlucky and injudicious was this Father in his charge of these frauds on the Jews, as to give an occasion onely for fixing them after all upon the Christians, and, in the opinion of some, even upon himself.

The learned and ingenious editor of his *Apologies and Dialogues*, who shews an inclination to defend him on all occasions where he is defensible, and on some even where he is not, yet is often forced to break out into a kind of astonishment at his ignorance, negligence, rashness, credulity, so gross in many instances, as to baffle all the art of criticism, nor to admit any certain rule of collecting his real sense. Yet *there are some still*, says he, *who extoll him, not onely as a most learned, but a most eloquent writer.*

Irenæus, whose character and doctrines come next to be considered, was, of all the Fathers whose works still remain to us, the most diligent collector and assertor of *Apostolic traditions.* And in truth, as far as his judgement and veracity may be relied upon, he seems to have been well qualified for that character; being acquainted, as he tells us, with several who had conversed familiarly with the Apostles, and curious also to inform himself of all the particular doctrines which they had ever taught by word of mouth. "He lived," says Mr. *Dodwell,* "so near to the times of the Apostles, as to be able to transmit their doctrines to posterity with certainty and fidelity, as they were delivered to him by oral tradition from their immediate successors and disciples." Yet *Photius,* one of the ablest critics of his own or any other age of the Church, has intimated a different character of him in the following short censure upon his writings; in which, *he thought it necessary,* he says, *to advertise the reader, that in some of them the purity of truth, with respect to ecclesiastical doctrines, is adulterated by his false and spurious reasonings.* But the following instances of the doctrines which he delivers as orthodox and *Apostolic,* will be the surest rule of determining his real character, as well as the proper degree of credit which may be due to his testimony.

He affirms then, *that our Saviour lived to an old age, or was fifty years old at the least,* at the time of his crucifixion; which he attempts to prove, first, from the reason of the thing; "that as Christ came to save all men, of all ranks and degrees, so it was necessary that he should pass through all the several stages of life, that he might be a pattern to them all: secondly, from the unanimous tradition and positive testimony of all the old men, who had lived with St. *John* and the other Apostles, from whom, he says, they all received this account, and constantly bore witness to the truth of it." Yet *this unanimous tradition*, so solemnly vouched by this venerable Father, is as certainly false as the Gospels are true. Dr. *Whitby*, after he has produced this same passage, cries out as it were with astonishment, "Behold here, according to *Irenæus*, how all the Elders of *Asia* testify with one voice, that they had received from St. *John* and the other Apostles a tradition concerning a fact manifestly false! behold an apostolic man, professing to prove from St. *John's Gospel*, things not onely contradictory to that Gospel, but to the articles of our Creed!" &c. The learned *Cave* also, in his Life of *Irenæus*, tells us, "that he was betrayed into this error,—partly from a mistaken report which he had somewhere picked up, (and it may be from his master, *Papias*,) and partly out of opposition to his adversaries, who maintained that our Saviour staid no longer upon earth than till the thirty-first year of his age; against whom the eagerness of disputation tempted him to make good his assertion from any plausible pretence," &c.

He asserts likewise the doctrine of the *Millenium*, in the grossest sense of it, from the same authority of a tradition, handed down to him by all the old men who had conversed with St. *John*, and heard him relate *what our Saviour himself used to teach concerning it:* of which he has recorded the following passage; "The days will come, in which there shall grow vineyards, having each 10,000 vine stocks; and each stock, 10,000 branches; each branch, 10,000 shoots; each shoot, 10,000 bunches; each bunch, 10,000 grapes; and each grape squeezed shall yield twenty-five measures of wine; and when any of the saints shall go to pluck a bunch, another bunch will cry out, I am a better, take me, and bless the Lord through me. In like manner a grain of wheat sown shall bear 10,000 stalks; each stalk 10,000 grains; and each grain 10,000 pounds of the finest flour; and so all other fruits, seeds, and herbs in the same proportion, &c. These words, says he, *Papias*, a disciple of St. *John*, and companion of *Polycarp*, an ancient man, testifies in writing in his fourth book, and adds, that they are credible to those who believe." The pious and cautious Dr. *Grabe* remarks on this occasion, "that what *Irenæus* says here about the stalks of grain, will be thought an argument of straw by those to whom such things appear incredible: but, that we ought not however either to deny or affirm any thing rashly." But *Eusebius* gives a a frank and clear solution of the matter, by informing us, that *Papias was a weak man, of a very shallow understanding, as it appeared from his writings, and by mistaking the meaning of the Apostles, imposed these silly traditions on* Irenæus, *and the greatest part of the ecclesiastical writers, who reflecting on the age of the man, and his near approach to the Apostles, were drawn by him into the same opinions.*

Irenæus affirms also, on the same authority of tradition, delivered to him by those who had received it from the Apostles, *that* Enoch *and* Elias *were translated into that very Paradise from which* Adam *was expelled*, to remain there till the consummation of all things: and that it was the same place into which St. *Paul* also was caught up. This is affirmed likewise by all the later Fathers, both *Greek* and *Latin*; induced to it, we may imagine, by the pretence of an Apostolical tradition: which yet, from the absurdity of it, must necessarily be as false as the rest above mentioned. *Feverdantius*, the learned editor of *Irenæus*, remarks upon this place; that tho' St. Austin *does not allow this opinion to be a point of faith, yet since* Irenæus *and all the primitive Fathers declare it to have been the doctrine of the Apostles, he cannot think it safe to believe otherwise.* And we must needs own him to be in the right, if, according to the principles of the Church of *Rome*, we can think the positive testimony of *Irenæus*, or the concurrent authority of all the Fathers, of weight enough to bear down the common sense and reason of mankind.

He asserts likewise very strongly, the fabulous story of the *Septuagint version*, with all the particulars already recited, of it's miraculous birth, and the separate cells, &c. To which he has added another, no less romantic; *that the sacred Scriptures were utterly destroyed in the* Babylonish *captivity, but restored again, after seventy years, by* Esdras, *in-*

spired by God for that purpose. And tho' in this also he was followed by all the principal Fathers of the succeding centuries, yet as Dr. *Prideaux* and other learned men have remarked, there is no better foundation for it than that *fabulous relation in the fourteenth chapter of the second Apochryphal book of* Esdras; a book too absurd even for the Romanists *themselves to admit into their canon:* and notwithstanding the authority of *Irenæus,* and of all the other Fathers who assert the same opinion, Mr. *Tillemont* declares *it to be very dangerous to religion, and tending extremely to weaken the authority of the Scriptures.* He intimates also more than once his belief *of angels mixing with the daughters of men:* where his editor takes notice that all the early Fathers were drawn into the same error, by the authority of the *Apochryphal book of* Enoch, cited by St. Jude. Yet as monstrous as this error was, it maintained its ground, as Dr. *Whitby* assures us, through the four first centuries; tho' St. *Chrysostom* treats it as *absurd and blasphemous, and all who espoused it as mad;* and *Theodoret* calls them *infatuated and very stupid.*

From some of the doctrines above mentioned, and particularly that of the *Millenium,* Mr. Chillingworth has proved against the *Romanists, that the Catholic Church, even in the earliest ages, and within thirty or forty years after the Apostles, was not infallible in matters of faith:* since all those absurdities were taught by the Fathers of those ages, not as their private opinions onely, but as doctrines of the Universal Church, derived immediately from the Apostles, and held so necessary, that those who held the contrary were hardly considered as real Christians: to which he adds the following remark; that if *Papias*, who first committed them to writing, *could either by his own error, or a desire to deceive, cozen the Fathers of the purest age in this, why not also in other things? Why not in twenty, as well as one? And why might not twenty others do it as well as he?*

As to *Irenæus's* manner of expounding the Scriptures, it is much the same with that of *Justin*, or rather, according to Dr. *Grabe*, with that of the age in which he lived: following no rule of criticism, nor giving any attention to the proper signification of words; but indulging a wild and enthusiastic fancy, in the invention of typical senses and forced allusions, utterly trifling and contemptible: *which those, who read the Fathers, must always bear in mind*, as a learned critic observes, *or they will be drawn into great and frequent errors.*

Treating of the distinction of animals into clean and unclean, he says, "The law foretold these things figuratively, by animals denoting men. Those who divide the hoof and chew the cud, it pronounces clean; those who do neither, unclean. Who then are clean? Those who believe in the Father and the Son. This is their firmness, or double hoof; and to meditate day and night on the laws of God, so as to be adorned with good works, is to chew the cud. But the unclean neither divide the hoof nor chew the cud; that is, neither have faith in God, nor meditate on his laws. This is the abomination of the Gentiles. But such as chew the cud, and do not divide the hoof, are unclean: this is a figurative description of the *Jews*," with much more to the same purpose. In which method of reasoning, as he followed *Barnabas*, and the Apostolic Fathers, so he was followed himself by the later writers; and especially by *Clemens of Alexandria*, who has copied this very passage.

Again, endeavouring to prove that the *Mosaic law* was to fill up the middle age of the world, between the natural law and the law of Christ, he says; "This was typically shewn by many things, but especially by *Thamar*, daughter-in-law to *Judas*. For when she was bringing out twins, one of them put out his hand the first; and as the midwife supposed him to be the first-born, she tied a scarlet string about his hand. But when this was done, he drew in his hand again, and his brother *Phares* came out first, and after him *Zara*, who had the mark. The Scripture clearly manifesting by it the people who had the scarlet sign; that is, the faith professed by those of the foreskin, or the uncircumcised; which was first shewn out in the Patriarchs, and then withdrawn, that it's brother might be brought out first, and then he be born afterwards, who had been shewn before, and was known by the scarlet sign; which is the passion of the Just one, præfigured from the beginning in *Abel*, described by the Prophets, but perfected in the last days by the Son of God."

His reasoning also upon the number of the Gospels is in the same strain. "It is impossible," says he, "that there could have been more or less than four. For there are four climates and four cardinal winds, and the Church is spread over the whole earth; but the Gospel is the pillar and foundation of the Church, and it's breath of life. The Church therefore was to have four pillars, blowing immortality from every quarter, and giving life to men," &c.

I have been the fuller in opening the characters and opinions of *Justin* and *Irenæus*, that I might save myself the trouble of inlarging in the same manner on the rest; especially as their characters will be sufficiently illustrated by the specimens of them occasionally interspersed in the sequel of this argument. But the later Fathers, generally speaking, do but copy the notions and even the blunders of these two. For as they are the earliest, who have left any considerable works behind them, so they are the first likewise in credit and authority with succeding ages, on the account of their piety, learning, and abilities; and the case was the same with the ancients as it is still with the moderns, that when any facts or doctrines have once been established by men of eminent character, they are usually taken upon trust by all who follow, till some new inquirer arises, who, not content with opinions imposed on him by chance or education, resolves to judge for himself, and to use his natural right and liberty of searching into the real grounds of them.

For instance, St. *Clemens of Rome* having alledged the ridiculous story of the *Phænix, as a type and proof of the resurrection,* all the later Fathers take it from him of course, and refer us to the same bird, not onely as really existing, *but as created on purpose by God, to refute the incredulity of the Gentiles* on the subject of this great article of our faith. Yet all the heathen writers, from whom they borrowed the story, from *Herodotus* down to their own times, treat it as nothing else but a mere fable. The case is the same with all the other facts and absurd doctrines above specified; of the *Millennium; of Angels debauching women, and begetting Dæmons; of the divinity of the Septuagint version; of the destruction of the sacred Scriptures in the* Babylonish *captivity*, &c. In all which, these two Fathers, whose principles I have been illustrating, were implicitly followed for a century or two at least by all their successors. *Irenæus* indeed stands single in his account of *the old age of Christ;* tho' confidently affirmed by him, on the pretended authority of all the Apostles; because it was evidently inconsistent with the history of the Gospels. But the later Fathers generally ran into a contrary extreme, and affirmed, what was maintained by the *Heretics onely of* Irenæus's *days, that our Lord preached but one complete year, and died at the age of thirty;* which, according to *Clemens* of *Alexandria*, was both foretold by the Prophets, and affirmed by the Evangelists. Whereas from the history of the Gospels, it is evident, that his ministry continued through *several successive Passovers*, or as Sir *Isaac Newton* has with great probability computed, through five; and that he died in his *thirty-fourth year*.

Now from what I have above collected, it is certain, that if a gross absurdity of opinions, and the belief of things impossible, be the proof of a weak mind; if expositions of the Scriptures, void of reason and common sense, betray a great want of judgement, then we may justly charge those defects upon these ancient fathers; from whose foolish reasonings, both in religion and morality, whole books have been compiled. Mr. *Dodwell,* one of their most zealous admirers, does not pretend to defend them on this head, but frankly owns, that their way of reasoning is *loose, sophistical and declamatory; far short of the solidity of the moderns, who excell them not onely in philosophy and learning, but in the knowledge of antiquity, and even of their own languages;* and all that he pleads for in favor of their interpretations, especially of the New Testament, is, *that they should not be wholly slighted, tho' they have but little sense in them, because they were agreeable to the custom or taste of those ages.*

As to the quæstion of their veracity, it may admit perhaps some debate, and it will probably be thought harsh in the opinion of many, to suspect men of such piety and sanctity of life either of the invention or the propagation of known forgeries. Yet there are many things so peremptorily affirmed, without any ground of truth or probability, by the two Fathers whose characters I have been considering, as to give us too much cause for such a suspicion: which, as we have seen above, has been actually charged on *Justin,* by men of learning, and may with equal reason be charged also on *Irenæus.* For what other account can be given of his frequent appeals to the tradition and testimony of the Apostles, for the support of so many absurd and incredible doctrines? If the doctrines themselves be false;

the pretended tradition of them could not possibly be true; and if we absolve *Irenæus* from the forgery it must be charged on somebody else more ancient still, and of authority enough to impose it upon him; and on whomsoever it may fall, it gives but a lamentable idea of those primitive ages, and primitive champions of the Christian cause.

Papias, who is supposed to have been the disciple of St. *John,* and Bishop of *Hierapolis,* is said to have given rise to most of the fabulous traditions, which obtained in those early days. Dr. *Whitby* joins *Irenæus* to him, and says: "It is very remarkable, that these two earliest writers of the second century, who, on the credit of idle reports and uncertain fame, have delivered to us things said to be done by the Apostles and their scholars, have shamefully imposed upon us, by the forgery of fables and false stories." But whoever forged the rest of the spurious traditions above recited, yet that which relates to *the old age of* Jesus, the most solemly attested of them all, and peculiar to *Irenæus,* may be fairly presumed to be his own forgery, because it was never embraced by any body else, and was singularly adapted to the argument, which he was then asserting in opposition to certain Heretics, called *Valentinians,* who allowed *but one intire year* to our Saviour's ministry.

But be that as it will; since the very earliest of all traditions, and the nearest to the fountain's head, are found to be so corrupt; it will demonstrate at least what a treacherous foundation they must be to build any opinion upon, and much more any article of our faith: which might be exemplified by many other instances from the history of the first centuries. For as soon as religious disputes began to infest the Church, the plea of Apostolical tradition was presently employed, as the most effectual to silence an adversary; and was taken up therefore and urged with equal confidence by all sides. And it is an argument indeed, which of all others seems the best calculated for the use of controversy: for wherever it meets with credit, it must necessarily have great weight; and where it happens even to find none, yet it cannot easily be confuted, as not being reducible to any clear test or fixed rule by which it may be tried. It is not therefore strange to find its authority carried so high, and in some cases magnified even above the Scriptures themselves, by all the dealers in controversy, from the earliest Fathers down to Dr. *Waterland*.

For example; in that most ancient and celebrated dispute between the eastern and western Churches, *about the time of holding their Easter*, St. *Polycarp*, Bishop of *Smyrna*, the disciple and immediate successor of the Apostles, and *Anicetus* his contemporary, the Bishop of *Rome*, severally alledged the authority of *Apostolic tradition* for their different practice, from which neither of them could be induced to depart. But *Papias*, as it is hinted above, the disciple of *Polycarp*, was the chief promotor and assertor of it: "as oft," says he, "as I met with any one who had conversed with the ancients, I always inquired very diligently after their sayings and doctrines: what *Andrew*, *Peter*, *Philip*, *John*, and the rest of our Lord's Apostles, used to teach. For I was persuaded that I could not profit so much by books, as by the voice of living witnesses." *Irenæus*, the scholar of *Papius*, who had learnt the use of it from his master, was likewise a zealous assertor of it. "If a dispute," says he, "should arise about any matter, tho' but of little moment, ought we not to have recourse to the most ancient Churches, in which the Apostles resided, and take from them what is certain and clear about the point in quæstion?" *Tertullian* declares it to be the onely weapon that can knock down an heretic; and in all such controversies advances it's authority above the Scriptures; nay, forbids any appeal to the Scriptures, as hurtful to the cause of truth. *We must not appeal to the Scriptures*, says he, *or trust the merits of the cause with them: in which there can either be no victory, or an uncertain one, or what is equivalent to uncertain.* And in this, Dr. *Waterland* declares, *that he seems to have judged well upon the prudential case, and like a wise and sagacious man with regard to the circumstances of those times.* And in another place the same learned Doctor observes, from the authority of *Irenæus*, that *Polycarp had converted great numbers to the Faith by the strength of tradition; being a sensible argument, and more affecting*, he says, *at that time, than any dispute from the bare letter of the Scripture could be.*

Here then we see in short the origin and history of tradition. *Papias*, a weak and silly man, who mistook the sense of the Apostles, was the first who made it his particular business to recommend the use of it, and for that purpose took the pains to collect all the unwritten facts and sayings of Christ and his Apostles, from the report of those who had conversed with them. These sayings, as *Eusebius* tells us, consisted of a number of *strange parables, and doctrines of our Saviour, with several other fabulous stories;* which the authority of so venerable a person, who had lived with the Apostles, imposed upon the Church for genuin: and the gravity of his scholar *Irenæus* confirmed and propagated to succeding ages: through which every one still added to the collection, whatever he thought useful to the particular cause or opinion that he favored. This account of the matter, deduced from the testimony of antiquity itself, confutes at once all the extravagant enconiums which our leading divines so lavishly bestow on those primitive Fathers and their traditions. For if the earliest and best vouched traditions of all which are transmitted to us be true, or at all to be regarded, it follows of course that we ought to receive the absurd doctrines above mentioned as articles of faith; *the fable of the Millennium; of the old age of Christ; of* Ænoch *translated into* Adam's *paradise;* with many more of the same stamp; which were all embraced by the earliest Fathers, and delivered to us, on the authority of the Apostles, by some of their immediate successors; and especially by those four, on whom Dr. *Waterland* lays the greatest stress; *Justin Martyr*, *Athenagoras*, *Irenæus* and *Clemens* of *Alexandria:* "eminent personages," as he says, "who florished within fifty, sixty, or at most ninety years from the Apostolic age. Whose nearness to the time, known fidelity, admirable indowments, ordinary and extraordinary, add great weight to their testimony or doctrine, and make it a probable rule of interpretation in the prime things." To which he subjoins in a marginal note, "that *Clemens*, tho' the latest of the four, yet testifies of himself, that he had received his doctrine from several disciples of the very chief Apostles; who had truly preserved the tradition of the blessed doctrine, as it came directly from the holy Apostles, *Peter*, *James*, and *John*." Notwithstanding all which, the Doctor could not but know, that this very *Clemens* holds as many absurd, unsound, and exploded doctrines, and deals as largely in the fabulous and apochryphal books of the primitive Christians, as any other Father whatsoever. These facts shew likewise the weakness of that argument, which the Doctor alledges for the truth of doctrines, from the *unanimity* with which they are asserted by the ancient writers. "This is the argument," says he, "which *Irenæus* and *Tertullian* insist much upon and triumph in, over the hæretics of their days; for it is highly unreasonable to suppose that Churches distant in place, and of different languages, and under no common visible head, should all unite in the same errors. Again, such unanimity could never come by chance, but must be derived from one common source: and therefore the harmony of their doctrine was in itself a pregnant argument of the truth of it." But if the unanimity of the primitive Fathers must be allowed to have so great a force as to evince the truth of any opinion, it would necessarily establish all those monstrous doctrines above specified; since it would be difficult to produce any other whatsoever in which there was so great an harmony among them, or so general a consent of the whole Church, through the three first centuries, and that intirely grounded upon the pretence of apostolic tradition.

But I cannot dismiss this article of the doctrines and opinions of these ancient Fathers, without taking notice of one which was universally received and believed through all ages of the primitive Church; *viz.*, "that there were a number of magicians, necromancers or conjurers, both among the Gentiles and the hæretical Christians, who had each their particular dæmons or evil spirits for their associates, perpetually attending on their persons, and obsequious to their commands; by whose help they could perform miracles, foretell future events, call up the souls of the dead, exhibit them to open view, and infuse into people whatever dreams or visions they thought fit." All which is constantly affirmed by the primitive writers and apologists, and commonly applied by them to prove the immortality of the soul.

"Let the powers of necromancy," says *Justin Martyr*, "and the evocations of human souls, and of boys especially, who had suffered violent deaths, and of those spirits whom the magicians call the inspirers of dreams and assessors, and the works which are performed by the skillfull in these arts, convince you that the souls of men exist still after death."

Lactantius, speaking of certain philosophers who held *that the soul perished with the body*, says, "they durst not have declared such an opinion in the presence of any magician, or if they had done it, he would have confuted them upon the spot, by sensible experiments; by calling up souls from the dead, and rendering them visible to human eyes, and making them speak and foretell future events."

The author of the book, called the *Recognitions of St. Clemens,* one of the most ancient and most learned of those many spurious pieces which were forged by the first Christians, affirms, "that *Simon Magus* confessed to one of his companions, that he wrought all his amazing works by the help of the soul of an healthy young boy, who had been violently put to death for that purpose, and then called up from the dead by ineffable adjurations, and compelled to be his assistant."

Irenæus, giving an account of the disciples of the same *Simon,* tells us, "that they lived lewdly, exercising magical arts, and using exorcisms, incantations, and love-charms, and industriously practising all other curious arts, by the assistance of their familiar spirits and inspirers of dreams." And speaking afterwards of the hæretic *Carpocrates* and his followers, he says, "These likewise practise magical arts, with incantations and love-charms, and have their assistant dæmons and inspirers of dreams, with all the other malevolent spirits."

"The magicians," says *Clemens of Alexandria,* "boast of dæmons, as the ministers of their impiety, reckoning them part of their family, and forcing them by their incantations to be the slaves of their will."

Tertullian declares of these dæmons, "that they had the power of inflicting horrible diseases both on the minds and bodies of men, and even cruel deaths; yet they frequently contrived to cure the disorders which they had wrought, in order to support the credit of their divinity, and the honor of their altars, and secure to themselves their proper food and nourishment from the rich steams and blood of the victims, which were offered to them." For this likewise, as monstrous as it is, was the common opinion of all the Fathers, taken as usual upon trust, from the authority of *Justin Martyr*, who was probably the inventor of it; "that the dæmons, after they had given themselves up to their lusts and lewd debaucheries with boys and women, began to want the rich fumes and the fat of sacrifices to strengthen them for the enjoyment of their lustfull pleasures."

Cyprian affirms, "that they commonly lay lurking within the statues and images of the heathen Deities; inspired the breasts of the southsayers; animated the fibres of the entrails of victims; directed the flight of birds, and the chances of lots; involving falsehood always with truth, and themselves sometimes deceived as well as deceiving others; disquieted the lives of men; disturbed their sleep; excited terrors in their minds, convulsions in their bodies; destroyed health and brought on diseases, so as to force people to worship them: that being filled and fatted by the steams of altars and burnt sacrifices, they might seem to cure the maladies which they had inflicted; whereas all the cure which they performed, was by ceasing onely to do hurt."

And as the whole system of Pagan idolatry was believed by the Fathers to have been managed by the craft and agency of dæmons, so the whole art of magic was supposed also to be carried on by the same powers, for the sake of deluding and destroying mankind. In the case of idolatry, they imagined them to assume the names, and to act the parts of the heathen Gods, and in magic to assume the forms of departed souls, and to appear under the names of those who were called up from the dead; and as such, to foretell future events, and answer to all quæstions which should be demanded of them. And the reason which they give why the souls called up from the dead were chiefly of those who had been put to a violent death, is, because such spirits were generally thought to be the most malevolent and revengeful, and ready to perpetrate the same acts of violence on others which they themselves had injuriously suffered.

Now the opinion which I have here explaned, is not only a proof of the grossest credulity, but of that peculiar species of it, which, of all others, lays a man the most open to the delusive arts of impostors. For a mind so totally possessed by superstitious fancies and disturbed by vain terrors, could not have either the judgement to discern, or the inclination to examine, or the courage even to suspect the pretensions of those vagrant jugglers, who in those primitive ages were so numerous, and so industriously employed in the affair of deluding their fellow creatures. Every man will perceive how easy it must have been to men of that class, whether

Heathens, Jews, or Christians, (for they are all allowed to have had such impostors among them,) to impose the tricks of their art as the effects of a supernatural power, on a multitude already persuaded that they lived on magic ground, exposed at every step to snares and charms, contrived by malicious spirits perpetually haunting them, and watching every unguarded moment to get possession both of their souls and bodies. And when pious Christians are arrived to this pitch of credulity, as to believe that evil spirits or evil men can work real miracles, in defiance and opposition to the authority of the Gospel, their very piety will oblige them to admit as miraculous whatever is pretended to be wrought in the defence of it, and so make them of course the implicit dupes of their own wonder-workers.

IV. I shall now procede, as I proposed, to take a particular review of all the several gifts, or miraculous powers, which were actually clamed and pretended to have been possessed by the primitive Church: which, according to the testimonies produced above, were, *the power of raising the dead; of healing the sick; of casting out devils; of prophecying; of seeing visions; of discovering the secrets of men; of expounding the Scriptures; of speaking with tongues.*

Sect. 1. As to the first, and the principal indeed of all miracles, that of raising the dead. It was frequently performed, as *Irenæus* affirms, *on necessary occasions; and men so raised had lived afterwards among them many years;* but it is very strange, that from the time of the Apostles there is not an instance of this miracle to be found in the three first centuries; except a single case, slightly intimated by *Eusebius*, from the books of *Papias;* which he seems to rank among the other fabulous stories delivered by that weak man.

It is certain, that if a miracle of so surprizing a nature had been so frequent as *Irenæus* affirms it to have been, or performed, as it were, in every parish or place where there was a Christian Church, it must have made great noise in the world, and been celebrated, not onely by the primitive Fathers, but by all the historians of those times. But it was so far from being commonly or openly effected, as every miracle should necessarily be which is wrought for the conversion of infidels, that all the enemies of the Gospel, as *Irenæus* himself confesses, constantly affirmed *the thing itself to be impossible.* A sure proof that they had never seen or known it to be done, unless in such a manner as carried with it a strong suspicion of fraud or collusion. Mr. *Dodwell* however, from this single authority of *Irenæus,* asserts the miraculous powers of the second century to be superior even to those of the first, or Apostolic age. *They raised the dead,* says he, *in the apostolic Churches, yet we have few examples of it in the genuin acts of the Apostles: but in* Irenæus's *days they raised not a few, but very often.* And in the same strain he runs through all the other miracles of the primitive times, and gives them the preference, in their number at least, to those of the Apostles; yet is forced to own, after all, that towards the end of the second century, and while *Irenæus* himself might be still living, this power of raising the dead was lost and vanished. For in the very same age, when one *Autolicus*, an eminent heathen, challenged his friend *Theophilus*, Bishop of *Antioch*, a convert and champion of the Gospel, *to shew him but one person who had been raised from the dead*, on the condition of turning Christian himself upon it, *Theophilus* discovers by his answer, that he was not able to give him that satisfaction. Upon which Mr. *Dodwell* remarks, *that the great number of persons who had been raised some years before, when the fact was common, were dead again for the second time in this interval;* which, for the sake of his hypothesis, he stretches as well as he can to *forty years*. But in truth, the fact itself, as delivered by *Irenæus*, seems to be utterly incredible on many accounts: 1st. That a case of so wonderful a nature should be common among them, yet not a single instance of it particularly described, or clearly attested in all history. 2dly. That it should be performed in every part of the world where there was a Church or assembly of Christians, yet all those who were not of that Church, and for whose sake it was chiefly performed, should be insisting all the while *that the thing itself was impossible*. 3rdly. That it should be common in the days of *Irenæus*, yet *Theophilus*, who lived at the same time, should not be able to alledge a single instance of it when challenged to it by his friend, whom he was laboring to convert, and who offered to be converted upon the proof of that fact. Lastly, That a power, of all others the most affecting and reputable to the

Church, should be withdrawn at a time when it's adversaries were defying them to shew any effects of it, and putting the merits of the controversy upon that very issue. All which circumstances laid together, must needs leave the strongest suspicion on the claim of the primitive Church, with regard to this prime miracle of *raising the dead.*

Sect. 2. The next gift said to have resided in it, is that *of healing the sick and curing all sorts of diseases:* in favor of which the ancient testimonies are more full and express; tho' with some variation concerning the method of cure. Some affirm that it was done by the *imposition of hands;* some, *by invoking the name of God and of Jesus, and reciting some story of his life;* and others, by the *use of oil,* which was consecrated by holy men, and dispensed to the people for the cure of their diseases. *Tertullian* tells us, "that a Christian called *Proculus* cured the Emperor *Severus* of a certain distemper by the use of oil: for which service that Emperor was favorable afterwards to the Christians, and kept *Proculus* as long as he lived in his palace." And St. *Jerom* affirms, "that *Hilarion the Monk* used to heal all the wounds of the husbandmen and shepherds with *consecrated oil;* and preserved the life of the son-in-law and daughter of an holy woman called *Constantia,* by anointing them with the same." Yet these cures, if true, might be accounted for probably without a miracle, by the natural power and efficacy of the oil itself, since in our days the bite of vipers, after inflaming a man's arm to a degree which threatened destruction to him, is known to have been checked and cured in a short time by the application of oil: which might perhaps have been the very case of *Hilarion's shepherds*. But be that as it will, the pretence of curing diseases by a miraculous power was so successfully maintained in the heathen world by fraud and craft, that when it came to be challenged by the Christians, it was not capable of exciting any attention to it among those who themselves pretended to the same power; which, tho' the certain effect of imposture, was yet managed with so much art, that the Christians could neither deny nor detect it; but insisted always that it was performed by *dæmons* or evil spirits, deluding mankind to their ruin: and from the supposed reality of the fact, inferred the reasonableness of believing what was more credibly affirmed by the Christians to be performed by the power of the true God. *We do not deny*, says *Athenagoras*, that *in different places, cities, and countries, there are some extraordinary works performed in the name of idols, from which some have received benefit, others harm.* But then he goes on to prove, that they were not performed by God, but by *Dæmons*. "If I should allow," says *Origen*, "that there is a Dæmon cunning in medicine, called *Æsculapius*, who cures diseases, yet I would say to those who are surprized at it, as well as at the prædictions of *Apollo*, that if the cure of diseases and prædiction of events be things of an indifferent nature, and which belong to bad as well as to good beings, shew me that those who cure and foretell are not bad, but good, and worthy to be held in a manner as Gods."

Whatever proof then the primitive Church might have among themselves of this miraculous gift, yet it could have but little effect towards making proselytes among those who pretended to the same gift; possessed more largely, and exerted more openly, than in the private assemblies of the Christians. For in the temples of *Æsculapius*, all kinds of diseases were believed to be publickly cured by the pretended help of that Deity: in proof of which there were erected in each temple *columns or tables of brass or marble*, on which a distinct narrative of each particular cure was inscribed. *Pausanius* writes, "that in the temple at *Epidaurus*, there were many columns anciently of this kind, and six of them remaining to his time, inscribed with the names of men and women who had been cured by the God, with an account of their several cases and the method of their cure: and that there was an old pillar besides, which stood apart, dedicated to the memory of *Hippolytus*, who had been raised from the dead." *Strabo* also, another grave writer, informs us, "that these temples were constantly filled with the sick, imploring the help of the God: and that they had tables hanging around them, in which all the miraculous cures were described." There is a remarkable fragment of one of these tables still extant, and exhibited by *Gruter* in his collection, as it was found in the ruins of *Æsculapius's* Temple, in the island of the Tyber, in Rome; which gives an account of *two blind men restored to sight by* Æsculapius, *in the open view, and with the loud acclamations of the people, acknowledging the manifest power of the*

God. Upon which the learned *Montfaucon* makes this reflection, that *in this are seen, either the wiles of the Devil, or the tricks of Pagan Priests, suborning men to counterfeit diseases and miraculous cures.*

Now tho' nothing can support the belief and credit of miracles more authentically than public monuments, erected in proof and memory of them at the time when they were performed; yet in defiance of that authority, it is certain that all those heathen miracles were pure forgeries contrived to delude the credulous multitude. And in truth, this particular claim of curing diseases miraculously, affords great room for such a delusion, and a wide field for the exercise of craft. Every man's experience has taught him, that diseases thought fatal and desperate, are oft surprizingly healed of themselves, by some secret and sudden effort of nature, impenetrable to the skill of man: but to ascribe this presently to a miracle, as weak and superstitious minds are apt to do,—to the prayers of the living, or the intercessions of the dead,—is what neither sound reason nor true religion will justify. Wherefore when the narratives of these pretended cures are delivered to us by partial and interested, or by weak and credulous men, they will always furnish reason to suspect that the relators were either deluded themselves, or willing to delude others: and unless we knew more precisely in this case the real bounds between nature and miracle, we cannot pay any great regard to such stories; especially when we are informed at the same time by the Christians themselves, that the same cures were performed also by knaves and impostors, of all sects and nations; by Heathens, Jews, and Heretics; which, according to the principles of those days, were ascribed either to the power of Dæmons, or to the magical force of amulets and charms.

Sect. 3. But the most eminent and celebrated of all the miraculous powers of the primitive Church was, the gift of *casting out Devils*, or the cure of *Dæmoniacs*. To this the ancient Fathers and apologists make the most frequent appeals; and on this they lay the greatest stress towards evincing the divinity of the Christian religion. It is not easy however to collect from their accounts what was the real case of these *Dæmoniacs*, and the proper nature of of their malady. The Fathers indeed themselves seem to have been fully persuaded, and labor to persuade every body else, that they were actually possessed and tormented by Devils, or evil spirits: yet many learned men of modern times have imagined them rather to have been affected by the *Epilepsy*, or *falling sickness*. Mr. *Dodwell* himself takes their case to have been of this kind, and curable *by the ordinary way of medicine*, as well as the extraordinary one of miracle. And it is certain, that the effects constantly ascribed to it seem to be nothing else but the ordinary symptoms of an *Epilepsy*, as they are described by the physicians. *Justin* speaks of them *as being thrown down always to the ground, by the Devils who possessed them*. And *Chrysostom*, in his elaborate consolation to *Stagirius*, who was also possessed, recites all the particulars of his case as they were related to him by a common friend: *the convulsion of his hands, the distortion of his eyes, the foam of his mouth, his horrid and inarticulate voice, the tremor of his body, and the long privation of his senses.* St. *Gregory*, of *Nyssa*, speaking of a woman also in the same case, says, *that groaning with a terrible and inarticulate voice, different from human, she fell flat on the ground, tearing her hair, her eyes distorted, her mouth foaming; nor did the Devil desist from strangling her, &c.* Then as to what these Fathers declare concerning their power of *lashing, burning, and tormenting* the Devils; and of their *groaning and howling* under the torture of the Christian exorcism, such an imagination might easily be conceived, from the strange convulsions of the body, and the hollow sighs and groans which commonly attend such fits. And the other circumstances likewise, so constantly attested by them all, concerning *the speeches and confessions of the Devils; their answering to all quæstions; owning themselves to be wicked spirits; telling whence they came and whither they were going, and pleading for favor and ease from the hands of the Exorcists;* may not improbably be accounted for, either by the disordered state of the patient, answering wildly and at random to any quæstions proposed; or by the arts of imposture and contrivance between the parties concerned in the act.

This, I dare say, will appear probable to every impartial reader, who, from the credulous and enthusiastic disposition of these Fathers, and their preconceived and erroneous notions about the origin and power of Dæmons, will be apt to conclude, that they were either induced by their prejudices to give too hasty a credit to these pretended possessions, or carried away by their zeal, to assist even in supporting a delusion which was useful to the Christian cause. And tho' this may sound harsh in the ears of many, it will not appear strange to those who have given any attention to the history of mankind; which will always suggest this sad reflection, that the greatest zealots in religion, or the leaders of sects and parties, whatever purity or principles they pretend to, have, seldom scrupled to make use of a commodious lie, for the advancement of what they call the truth. And with regard to these very Fathers, there is not one of them, as an eminent writer of ecclesiastical history declares, who made any scruple in those ages of using *the hyperbolical style*, to advance the honor of God and the salvation of men. For it is certain, that the greatest part of the wonderfull things which they relate, are in themselves utterly incredible; and such of them as happen to be the most distinctly described, carry always the greatest marks of art and contrivance for the sake of serving some particular purpose. For example, *Tertullian*, who was an utter enemy to plays and public shews in the Theaters, wrote a book to deter all Christians from frequenting them, in which he tells the following story: "An example happened," says he, "as the Lord is witness, of a woman who went to the Theater and came back with a Devil in her; whereupon when the unclean spirit was urged and threatened in the office of exorcising, for having dared to attack one of the faithfull, *I have done nothing,* replied he, *but what is very fair, for I found her on my own ground.*" He adds a second story still more dreadfull, "of another woman, who, in the very night, after she had seen a tragedy in the Theater, had her winding-sheet shewn to her in a vision, in which she was reproached by name, with the Tragedian, whom she had been seeing, and did not live above five days after."

Now in this last case, it is not improbable, that a poor weak woman, who went to sleep under the consciousness of a grievous sin committed by her, might, by the terrors of a dream, be thrown into a disorder that put an end to her life. But in the first, tho' God himself is appealed to for the truth of it, yet when we reflect on the principles of those times, and the particular warmth of *Tertullian's* zeal, we cannot but suspect, that the smart answer of the Devil, was contrived to enforce, what he was so warmly inculcating, the horrible sin and dangerous consequence of frequenting the public theaters.

It is very remarkable, that all the Fathers, who lay so great a stress on this particular gift of casting out devils, yet allow the same power both to the *Jews* and the Gentiles, as well before as after our Saviour's coming. *Justin Martyr,* in his dialogue with *Trypho* the *Jew,* says, "that all Devils yield and submit to the name of *Jesus,* when they would not to any other name of their Kings, Prophets, or Patriarchs; yet if any should exorcise them in the name of the God of *Abraham, Isaac,* and *Jacob,* they would in like manner submit. For your Exorcists, adds he, as well as the Gentiles, use this art in exorcising, together with certain fumes and ligatures." And the *Jews,* says *Irenæus,* even now, by this same invocation of the name of God, drive away Devils.

Origen, in his dispute with *Celsus,* asserting the descent of the *Jews* from *Abraham, Isaac,* and *Jacob,* says, "that these names joined to that of God, have such power, that not onely their own nation use them in their prayers, and in casting out devils, but all other Inchantors and Magicians whatsoever; and that in magical books, the same invocation and use of God's name is often found, as peculiar to the art and effectual against Devils." And speaking of *Abraham's* great merit, he observes, "that it is not *Moses* onely who celebrates it, but that many of those, who charm or drive out Devils, call upon the God of *Abraham,* without knowing even who *Abraham* was." Again, "if a man," says he, "invoke or exorcise by the name of the God of *Abraham, Isaac,* and *Jacob,* the Devils will obey, and do what they are commanded; but if he translate those names, according to their meaning, into any other language, they will have no force at all. The same, adds he, is true of the word, *Sabaoth,* so much used in incantations; if it be applied in it's original *Hebrew,* it is effectual; but if translated into another tongue, so as to put for it *the Lord of Hosts,* it avails nothing, if we believe the skillfull in these matters."

Josephus writes, "that *Solomon* was particularly instructed by God in the art of casting out Devils, for the benefit of mankind; and that he left behind him a receit of those charms and exorcisms, by which he used to drive them out: which same method was the most effectual even to his time. For I saw, says he, one of my countrymen, *Eleazar*, casting out Devils, in the presence of *Vespasian*, his sons and officers, and a multitude of soldiers. His method was this: he applied to the nose of a person possessed, a ring, which had a certain drug or root under the seal of it, which *Solomon* had prescribed; and so, by the smell of the ring, he drew out the Devil through the nostrils of the patient, who fell presently to the ground; upon which he adjured the Devil never to return, rehearsing the name of *Solomon*, with certain charms, which he had composed and left behind him; and being desirous to convince the company that he was really indued with this power to which he pretended, he placed a certain cup or vessel filled with water at a little distance from the person possessed, and commanded the Devil, as he was going out of him, to overturn the cup, so as to give the spectators a manifest proof that he had quitted the body of the man." Which shews, in contradiction to what *Justin Martyr* affirmed above, that besides the name of *Jesus*, the Devils were subject likewise to that of *Solomon*.

Now it will be granted, I suppose, by all men of sense, that these *Jewish* and Gentile Exorcists were mere knaves and impostors; who, by their tricks and false miracles, contrived to delude the credulous multitude, in order to acquire gain or power to themselves, and to keep their people firm to the

Jewish or heathenish rites, in opposition to the Christian. *Ulpian*, the lawyer, speaks of *Exorcism* in general, as a term of art used by impostors; by who he is supposed by some to mean the *Jewish*, by others the *Christian Exorcists*. But *Tertullian*, and all the Fathers in general declare, that these magicians and wandering jugglers performed many wonderfull things, above the force of human power, which they wholly ascribe to the assistance of Dæmons. And if they were so far deluded by those *Jewish* and Gentile pretenders, as to take such senseless charms, and tricks of legerdemain, for the effects of a supernatural power, their prejudices would operate much more strongly in favor of their own Impostors, who had taken up the same trade: or if they saw through the cheat of the Gentile practitioners, yet on account of the credit which they had gained with the people, and the difficulty of detecting the fraud, they might think it convenient perhaps to oppose one cheat to another, and set up rival powers of their own, in opposition to those of their adversaries, in hopes of beating them at their own weapons.

For it is very hard to believe what *Origen* declares above, that the Devils, for the sake of doing the greater mischief to men, *used to possess and destroy their cattel.* In confirmation of which St. *Jerom* has related a most ridiculous story, in his life of St. *Hilarion* the Monk; where, after a narrative of many cases of Devils expelled by that saint from the bodies of men, he adds, " but it is to little purpose to talk of men; brute animals also were dayly brought to him, mad or possessed; among the rest a *Bactrian Camel*, of an enormous size, which had already destroyed many people: above thirty men were employed to drag him along with the strongest ropes. His eyes were bloody, his mouth foaming, his tongue rolling and swoln, and his strange roaring above all terrors. The old man ordered it to be let loose, upon which all who were about him ran away immediately. The saint came forward alone, and in the *Syriac* tongue, said, *Thou dost not affright me, Devil, with all that bulk of body: thou art one and the same in a little fox, or in a camel:* and so he stood firm with his arm stretched out; and as the beast advanced towards him, furious and ready to devour him, it presently fell down with it's head to the ground, so that all present were amazed at the sudden change from so great a fierceness to such a tameness. Upon which the old man took occasion to teach them, that the Devil used to seize cattel out of his hatred to men, to whom he bore so great a grudge as to wish not onely that they, but that all which they had, might perish." To this story I cannot forbear adding, what is likewise affirmed by the same *Jerom*, of the same *Hilarion*, that *he was so full of the power of the Holy Spirit, as to be able to discover from the smell of the bodies and cloaths of men, or of any thing else, which they had but touched, to what particular Dæmon, or to what vice they were severally subject.* Now, tho' this good Father invokes *the assistance of the Holy Spirit in his attempt to describe a life so wonderfull*, yet all who read it must needs be persuaded, that out of his zeal and warm affection to the monkish order, which he professed, and from a desire to advance it's credit in the world, he either wholly invented, or at least willfully propagated all these extravagant tales, which he himself could not possibly believe. "The time," says he, "would fail me, if I should attempt to relate all the wonderfull works that were performed by him: wherefore by the influence of his example, *innumerable monasteries began to be founded through all Palæstine;* and all the Monks ran eagerly to *Hilarion,* &c." This was the real purpose of St. *Jerom's* zeal; this the fruit of his fictitious miracles. But to return to the *Dæmoniacs.* Since this gift of casting out Devils is what the Fathers, as I have said above, lay the greatest stress upon, and to which they make the most frequent appeals, it may be proper to strengthen what I have already been declaring upon it, by a few particular observations, which I would recommend to the attention of the reader.

1*st,* That there is such an uniformity in all the primitive accounts of them, tho' given by different Fathers and in different ages, *of the Devils being scourged, burned, and tortured by the Christian Exorcists; and of their howlings, discourses, and confessions,* that they all seem to have been cast in the same mould; and to have been the copies rather of one original story, transcribed by the later writers from the earlier, than the natural descriptions, of what each of them had severally seen, at different times, and in distant places.

2*dly,* That the persons thus possessed, and in

whom the Devils used to hold discourses, were called by the primitive Christians, 'Εγγαςριμύθοι or *Ventriloquists;* because they were believed *to speak out of the belly, thro' the navel.* Thus in a book ascribed to *Justin Martyr,* containing a number of Quæstions with answers to them, for the use of the *Orthodox,* one of the questions is this; "if all the arts of delusion are abolished by the coming of Christ, how comes it to pass, that Dæmons still speak by those who are called *Ventriloquists,* and that they do not make Christianity ridiculous and contemptible, by shewing forth the works of imposture and uttering oracular prædictions in the bodies of Christians?"

Now many of us have seen, and may still see perhaps at this day, a sort of these *Ventriloquists,* who by a particular formation of their organs, managed by art and practice, could speak in such a manner as to persuade the company that the voice did not procede from them, but from some invisible being; which they could direct likewise so as to make it seem to come from what part of the room they pleased; by which means, weak and ignorant people have been terrified almost out of their senses, believing it to be the *voice of a Spirit or Dæmon.* If we suppose then, that there were any Artists of this kind among those ancient Christians, as there undoubtedly were among the ancient Gentiles, it is easy to imagine, what strange and surprizing feats might be performed, by a correspondence between the *Ventriloquist* and the *Exorcist,* so as to delude the most sensible and sagacious of their audience, prepossessed with the belief of these diabolical possessions, and void of all suspicion that such effects could possibly be produced by any human art or natural cause.

3dly. From the testimony of Antiquity itself it is evident, that many of their Dæmoniacs could not possibly be cured by all the power of the Exorcists; and that the cures, which are pretended to have been wrought on any, were but temporary, and appear to have been the cessation rather of a particular fit, or access of the distemper, than the real expulsion of a Dæmon. This may be clearly collected from the method of treating them in the primitive Church, as it was regulated by several Canons and rules, made for that purpose by Bishops and Councils, injoining, "that they should not be received to baptism, but in the intervals of their disorder; nor to the Communion, unless they shewed signs of piety and sobriety, so as not to expose and blaspheme the mysteries; in which case they might communicate now and then: that they should never be ordained or taken into any order of the Clergy, nor allowed to pray in common with the congregation, but be produced always separately, and commanded onely to bow down their heads, while the rest of the Assembly were offering up a prayer for them." In different Churches however, a different discipline was observed with regard to them; for in some they were admitted to baptism, and even to dayly communion; by which means many are affirmed to have been relieved when all the arts of the Exorcists had been tried upon them in vain. Now these cases manifestly shew, that this celebrated gift, as it was managed by the primitive Church, was not able to work an absolute cure, or to drive out the Devils so effectually, as to reduce the patients to a permanent state of sanity, so as to render them ordinarily capable, either of baptism, or the Eucharist, or of joining even with the congregation in the dayly prayers of the Church. Whence we may reasonably conclude, that it was nothing else but a false mimickry of that genuin power which was exercised by our Lord, and conferred afterwards on his Apostles: a power which never did it's work by halves, or left it's cures imperfect. For, as we learn from the Gospel, *Mary Magdalen*, from whom *seven Devils* were cast out, continued ever after in her sober senses, accompanying and ministring on all occasions to our Lord, to the time of his death: and the man also, out of whom a *Legion* of them was ejected, was restored at once to perfect health, both of mind and body, and sent away to proclame in *Decapolis*, and the neighbouring country, the miraculous cure which *Jesus* had wrought upon him.

4thly. There is another circumstance belonging to these primitive Dæmoniacs, of which the reader perhaps may desire some farther explication; I mean the great numbers of them, which appear to have subsisted in those early ages: whose chief habitation was within a part of the Church, allotted to them for that purpose; in which, as in a kind of Hospital, they were committed to the care of the Exorcists; whose business it was, "to pray over them on some occasions, and to provide their dayly food, and keep them employed in some bodily exercise and innocent business, of sweeping the Church and the like, to prevent the more violent agitations of Satan, and lest he should be tempted by their idleness to renew his attacks upon them." Which method of relieving so miserable a tribe of helpless mortals, will account for the numbers with which the Churches were stored, as well as for the confidence of those challenges made to the Heathens by the Christian Apologists, to come and see at any hour, and any warning, how they could *torment, and lash, and burn, and drive the evil spirits* out of them; while they kept such numbers of them in constant pay, always ready for the shew; tried and disciplined by their Exorcists to an habit of groaning and howling, and to give proper answers to all questions which should be demanded of them.

It is observable also in the last place, that this power of *exorcising Dæmoniacs or casting out Devils*, which had hitherto been in the hands onely of the meaner sort of the Christian layety, was put under the direction of the Clergy, by the *Council of Laodicea*, about the year of Christ three hundred and sixty seven, in which it was decreed, that *none should be Exorcists but those who were appointed by the Bishop.* After which appropriation of it, as Mr. *Whiston* informs us, "few or none of the clergy, nor indeed of the layety, were any longer able to cast out Devils; so that the old Christian exorcism or prayer for the *Energumens* in the Church, began soon after to be omitted as wholly useless." Which sudden failure of so eminent a gift seems to be ascribed by him to that fatal step of this *unhappy*

Council, as he calls it; as if, by their presumptuous attempt to controul the divine power, they had provoked God to withdraw it. But tho' this solution of the case may be agreeable to the character and principles of that very learned and pious writer, yet it is more agreeable to reason and the experience of mankind to suppose, that the licencious abuse of this imaginary power by the many false and impudent pretensions of crafty impostors on the one hand, and wrong-headed Enthusiasts on the other, had brought such scandal on Christianity itself, that the Clergy were forced at last to interpose, and take the affair into their own hands. For that this was really the case, is manifestly shewn by the event; since the exercise of this gift was no sooner subjected to any regulation, even by those who favored and desired to support it, than it gradually decreased and expired.

Sect. 4. The next miraculous gift ascribed to the primitive Church, is that of *Prophetic visions and extatic trances, and the discovery of men's hearts;* for these seem to be the fruit of one and the same spirit; which exerted itself chiefly about the end of the second and the beginning of the third century, through *Tertullian's and Cyprian's* days. "The divine censure," says *Cyprian*, "does not cease to chastise us, neither by night nor by day; for besides nightly visions, even boys among us are filled with the Holy Ghost, and, in fits of ecstasy, see, hear, and utter things, by which the Lord thinks fit to admonish and instruct us." This ecstasy was a temporary madness or loss of senses, and is called by *Tertullian, the spiritual virtue in which prophecy consists. Suidas* says, that of all the kinds of fury or madness, that of the Poets and Prophets was alone to be wished for.

Mr. *Dodwell* observes, "that visions were peculiar to the young, dreams to the old; because it required a great strength of body to support the violence of such divine agitations." *Philo,* the Jew, treating of the same ecstasies with which the Patriarchs and Prophets of the Old Testament used to be affected, reasons thus, "the human mind," says he, "is symbolically called the Sun by *Moses;* while our mind therefore shines and exerts itself within us, spreading as it were a meridian light through the Soul, we are then in our right senses, without any divine influx: but when the mind goes down, then a divine ecstasy and prophetic madness fall upon us; for when the divine light shines, the human sets; and when that sets, this again rises; and this is what usually happens to the prophetic race; for the mind is driven out of us when the divine spirit comes in, and when this again quits us, the other returns; for it is not fit that mortal should cohabit with immortal.

From these testimonies we may collect, that the Prophecy of the Primitive Church by *vision* or *ecstasy,* was of the same kind, as to it's outward appearance, with *that divination by fury,* as it was called among the Gentiles, which was practised by the *Delphic Pythia* and *Cumæan Sibyl,* when agitated by the pretended power and instinct of the God.

Of which *Cicero* says, in way of raillery, "what authority can that madness have which you call divine; that a wise man should not be able to foresee what a madman can; and that he who has lost all human senses, should presently acquire divine ones."

Montanus the heretic, and his female associates, seem to have been the authors of these prophetic trances towards the end of the second century; and acquired great credit by their *visions and ecstasies,* in which they acted their part so well, by feigned distortions and convulsive agitations of the body, as to appear to be out of their senses; and in those fits, uttered many wild prophecies and predictions, which they imposed upon the people for divine revelations; and by affecting at the same time a peculiar sanctity and severity of discipline, gathered a great number of disciples, who first raised and propagated that spirit of enthusiasm in the Church, which subsisted in it for near a century, under the title of *vision and prophecy,* and then gradually sunk into utter contempt.

Tertullian, a writer of this enthusiastic turn, severe in his manners, and stiff in his opinions, wrote with great vehemence against Plays and Shews; in which, as we have seen above, he made great use of visions towards enforcing his argument. He wrote another book to prove, *that it was a Sin for a Soldier to wear a garland or crown on any occasion, and that a Christian should rather suffer martyrdom than submit to it;* and in a third book, he affirms it to be rank idolatry *to deck their doors with garlands or flowers on Festival days, according to the custom of the Heathens;* "and calls the name of God to witness, that he knew a person who had been grievously chastised in a vision, because his servants, even without his knowledge and in his absence, had crowned the door with flowers on some occasion of public joy." He wrote a treatise likewise to prove the soul of man to be *corporeal and of human shape;* and for the truth of his opinion, appeals to his ecstatic maid abovementioned, of whom he tells this story, that "as he happened to be discoursing on the nature of the soul, she fell into one of her trances; and as soon as the service was over, and the people dismissed, she came as usual to relate to him what she had seen; which was always carefully taken down in writing in order to be examined; when she declared, that there was shewn to her among other things an human soul in bodily form, yet so as to appear to be a spirit; not of a void and empty quality, but what might even be handled, tender and lucid, of an airy color, and in all points of human shape." Which wild dream of a frantic, or fiction rather of a silly woman, this Father applies, as the testimony of God himself, to evince the certainty of his opinion. Lastly, in another book, written to prove that women ought always *to wear a veil,* he declares, *that God, in a vision to a certain sister, had prescribed to her, by a special revelation, the exact length and measure of the veil."*

Now it is easy to imagine, how *Tertullian* might be imposed upon by the craft of these extatic visionaries, and by the warmth of his temper and force of his prejudices, be drawn to espouse any delusion that flattered his particular zeal and favorite opinions. But it is difficult to account for the same conduct in his scholar *Cyprian*; a man of a more acute head and sober mind, but fond of power and Episcopal Authority; whose character would tempt us to suspect, that he was the inventor rather than the believer of such idle stories, and the director rather than the dupe of senseless visionaries. Yet in all quæstionable points of doctrine or discipline, which he had a mind to introduce into the Christian worship, we find him constantly appealing to the testimony of *heavenly visions and divine revelations. It is certain*, says Mr. *Dodwell, that all things of great moment, which related to the public state of the Church, were foretold to him in visions.* For instance, in a letter to *Cæcilius*, he declares, that he had received a divine admonition *to mix water with wine in the Sacrament of the Eucharist, in order to render it effectual.* In another to the Clergy, concerning certain Priests who had restored some lapsed Christians too hastily to the Communion of the Church, he threatens them to execute *what he was ordered to do against them, in a vision, if they did not desist.* He makes the same threat to one *Pupianus*, who had spoken ill of him, and withdrawn himself from his communion; where his editor *Rigaltius* makes this remark, "that the argument of visions and divine revelations, which *Cyprian* so frequently uses, is a weapon of great force in the hands of so good a man, otherwise a vain and contemptible one; since crafty Sophists might easily invent such visions, in favor of any cause, to delude the simple and unwary."

In a letter likewise to the Clergy and the people, *Cyprian* tells them, "how he had been admonished and directed by God, to ordain one *Numidicus* a Priest: who by his persuasive exhortations had sent a large number of Martyrs before him to the other world, either stoned or burnt to death; and beheld even with joy, the wife of his bosom burnt together with the rest; being himself also left for dead, half burnt and buried in stones, till he was found scarce alive, and carried off by the piety of his daughter, and so restored to the world against his will. But the Lord had now signified the cause of it; that he might add him to the Priesthood of his Church." In another letter he recommends to them one *Celerinus*, whom he had ordained a lecturer: *whose modesty*, he says, *had been over-ruled and compelled by a divine vision, to accept that office.* Where *Rigaltius* once more reflects, *on the great diligence of* Cyprian, *in making such use of visions.* But *Cyprian* himself suggests the reason of it, in the Epistle immediately preceding, addressed likewise to the clergy and the people, concerning one *Aurelius*, whom he had ordained a lecturer, by a *divine admonition*, without calling them together and consulting with them in common, concerning the character and merit of the candidate, as it was the custom of those days in all *clerical ordinations*; for which he excuses himself by saying, that there was no occasion, in the present case, *to wait for human testimonies, when the divine suffrage had already been signified.* This then seems to be the meaning of *Cyprian's diligence in the use of visions*, that whenever he thought fit to exert his Episcopal authority, *without the previous consent of his Clergy and people*, he might obviate their murmurs by alledging a divine command for it.

But the most memorable effect of any of his visions was, his flight and retreat, when he withdrew himself from his Church, in the time of persecution. A step which gave great scandal, and seems to have been considered by the Clergy of *Rome*, in a public letter written upon the subject of it, to the Clergy of *Carthage*, as a desertion of his post, and pastoral duty. So that it is no wonder to find *Cyprian* himself, as well as his Apologist *Pontius*, the writer of his Life, so sollicitous to excuse it. "There is no doubt, says *Rigaltius*, but that the severity of his master *Tertullian*, who wrote a book against all flight in time of persecution, raised such scruples and shame in the mind of *Cyprian*, as made him labor hard to wipe off that disgrace; as the pains and perplexity of his Advocate *Pontius* likewise shew." They both of them therefore affirm, "that he was commanded to retire, *by a special revelation from heaven:* and that his flight was not the effect of any other fear but that of offending God, and that his mind, wholly devoted and subservient to the admonitions of God, was persuaded, that, if he had not obeyed the Lord, when he commanded him to retreat, he should sin even by suffering martyrdom." Yet this plea was nothing else without doubt, but a mere fiction, contrived for the purpose of quieting the scandal, that was raised by his flight, and is in effect confuted by himself in another letter to the Clergy, in which he declares, "that it was the advice and authority of one *Tertullus*, which prevailed with him to withdraw himself from a place, where his life was so much sought for: wherefore he desires them to perform all the functions of his office for him during his retreat, since their persons were not exposed to so much envy and danger as his would be."

Dionysius, Bishop of *Alexandria*, who lived in the same age, has left the same story likewise concerning himself, and swears to the truth of it: that in the time of a persecution, he was commanded by God in a vision to retire from *Alexandria*, and was wonderfully preserved and guarded by him in his retreat. *And shall we not believe a most holy Bishop*, says Mr. Dodwell, *even upon his oath?* The same *Dionysius* affirms likewise that he had another vision, upon the subject of *reading heretical books*, about which he had some scruples, till a *voice from heaven expressly injoined him to read them all without reserve, because he was able to examine and confute them.* This reminds me of a vision also which St. *Jerom* declares to have been given to himself, about a century after; *in which he was dragged to the tribunal of Christ, and terribly threatened, and even scourged for the grievous sin of reading secular and profane writers,* Cicero, Virgil, *and* Horace; *whom for that reason he resolved never to take into his hands any more:* upon which *Ruffinus* rallies him with great spirit and smartness,

ting and publishing so silly a lie. And it
ls be thought strange, that God should in-
arieties to his saints and servants; should
one Father to read heretical books because
e to confute them, yet forbid it afterwards
who was full as able to confute them as
ssor. But if *Jerom's* vision deserved to be
his contemporaries as a fiction, I see no
her from the nature of the thing, or the
is made of it, or the characters of the per-
rned, why the visions of Cyprian and Dio-
ld not merit the same treatment.

credible soever these visions might appear
erality of Christians in those days, yet
many at the same time, as *Cyprian* him-
es, who contemned and made a jest of
s mere illusions and impertinent fancies:
vere a sort of men, he says, *who would*
ve any thing against a Priest, than believe

of the Dialogues commonly ascribed to
Christians seem to be ridiculed on the
their *fasting and watching whole nights in*
prayers, as if they could infuse by that
'ever sort of dreams or visions they thought
there is a passage so applicable to this re-
narrative of the Martyrdom of
nake us almost imagine that the
o it. The narrative was drawn
ad accompanied the Martyr from
se thoughts for several months
oyed on nothing else but the sub-

ject of his martyrdom, and it concludes thus: "These things were done on the 13th of the Kalends of January; *Sura and Synecius* being the second time Consuls of Rome; of which we ourselves were eye-witnesses. And the night following, as we were watching with tears in the house, and praying to God with bended knees, that he would impart to us weak men some assurance of what was done, [with regard to the Martyr,] it happened, that falling into a slumber, some of us, on a sudden, saw the blessed *Ignatius* standing before us and embracing us; others beheld the blessed Martyr praying for us; others, as it were dropping with sweat, as if just come from his great labor, and standing by the Lord: which when we saw, being filled with joy, and comparing the visions of our dreams with each other, we glorified God, the giver of all good, and being assured of the blessedness of the saint, we have made known unto you both the day and the time, that being assembled together, according to the time of his martyrdom, we may communicate with the combatant and most valiant Martyr of Christ."

But to declare freely what I think: whatever ground there might be in those primitive ages, either to reject or to allow the authority of those visions, yet from all the accounts of them that remain to us in these days, there seems to be the greatest reason to suspect that they were all contrived, or authorized at least, by the leading men of the Church, for the sake of moderating and governing with more ease the unruly spirit of the populace, in those times of danger and difficulty. For they are generally applied to excuse the conduct of particular persons, in some instances of it liable to censure; or to enforce some particular doctrine or discipline, warmly pressed by some, and not well relished by others; or to confirm things not onely trifling and frivolous, but sometimes even superstitious and hurtfull to true religion.

I have already observed, that it was the heretic *Montanus*, who first gave a vogue to prophetic visions and ecstacies in the primitive Church. But when his pretensions came afterwards to be suspected and decried, it is remarkable that those who undertook to expose and confute them, employed such argument against his prophecy, as seemed to shake the credit of all prophecy. For whereas the *Montanists* delivered their prophecies always in *ecstacy*, or with loss of senses, it was then urged against them, "that this was the proof of a diabolical spirit; that the true prophets never had such fits; never lost their senses; but calmly and sedately received and understood whatever was revealed to them." And *Epiphanius* makes this the very criterion or distinguishing character between a true and false prophet; *that the true had no ecstasies, constantly retained his senses, and with firmness of mind apprehended and uttered the divine oracles.* St. *Jerom* also declares, *that the true prophets never spake in ecstasy, or madness of heart, like* Montanus *and his mad women,* Prisca and Maximilla, *but understood what they delivered, and could speak or hold their tongues whenever they pleased, which those who spake in ecstasy could not do. Eusebius* also mentions a book of one *Miltiades*, written against *Montanus*, the purpose of which was, to prove *that a prophet ought not to speak in ecstasy*. Yet from the testimonies collected above, we have seen, that before the *Montanists* had brought those *ecstasies* into disgrace, the prophecy of the orthodox, as well as that of the heretics, was declared to have been exerted in *ecstasy*. And it appears to have been the current opinion in those earlier days, that the prophets also of the Old Testament received and uttered their revelations in *ecstasy*.

Athenagoras expressly affirms it, and says, "that while they were under the divine impulse, they were transported out of their senses, and delivered in ecstacy what was inspired, being mere organs of the Holy Spirit, just as a pipe or flute is of him who blows into it." *Justin Martyr* speaks of them in the same strain, "that the Spirit of God descending from above, made use of them as of an instrument, just as the quill strikes the harp or lyre, to revele to us the knowledge of divine and heavenly things." *Tertullian* also declares, "that he who has the Spirit within him, must necessarily be deprived of his senses, especially whenever he beholds the glory of God, or when God speaks by him, as being then overshadowed by the divine power."

Again, *Montanus's* associate, *Maximilla*, gave out *that the gift of prophecy was to cease with her*, and no other prophet was to arise after her. In answer to which, the orthodox asserted, *that the true spirit of prophecy could never fail or cease in the Church, till the consummation of all things*. In which, as Mr.

Dodwell owns, "the ancients argued rashly, and were mistaken in their notion of the perpetuity of prophecy; since *Eusebius*, who made it his business to explore and deduce the succession of those prophetic gifts, intimates that they were ceased and vanished in his days:" that is, about the middle of the fourth century.

Since we are now considering the miracles of the *Cyprianic* age, I cannot forbear taking notice of two or three of those wonderfull stories, which *Cyprian* himself attests, in that *magnificent treatise*, as it was called, concerning *the lapsed* Christians, who, in the time of persecution, had been induced by the terrors of present death or tortures to deny Christ, or offer incense to an idol. "There was a man," says he, "who went up voluntarily to the Capitol to deny the Lord; and when he had denied him, was presently struck dumb.—A woman also, who, after her lapse, had the impudence to go to the baths, was there seized by an unclean spirit, and thrown to the ground, and with her teeth tore that tongue with which she had been either talking or feeding impiously; and so became her own executioner; for she died not long after in great anguish and torments of her bowels." He introduces the next story more solemnly, by declaring that he himself was present and an eye-witness of it. "Certain parents," says he, "too solicitous for their own safety, and flying from persecution, left an infant daughter to the care of a nurse; who carried it presently to the magistrates. These being then assembled with the people before an idol, and seeing the child not yet old enough to eat flesh, gave it a piece of bread dipt in wine, being the remains of what had been offered to the idol. The mother, ignorant of the fact, within a short time after took her daughter home again: but the child was yet no more able to discover the crime committed, than she was before to understand or to hinder it. The mother brought her therefore to us at the sacrament, while we knew nothing of the matter. But the child being now mingled with the saints, and impatient of the service and prayers, began to be seized, sometimes with fits of crying, sometimes with tortures of the mind, and, as if it had been upon the rack, betrayed by all the signs which it's tender age could give, a sense of guilt and consciousness of the fact. The service being ended, when the Deacon began to give the cup to all present, and it came to the child's turn, the little one, by divine instinct, turned away it's face, held it's lips close shut, and refused the cup: the Deacon persisted, and poured a little down it's throat, tho' by force. Upon this, convulsions and vomitings insued. The Eucharist could not stay in a body and mouth so defiled: the consecrated potion of the Lord's blood burst out of it's polluted bowels. So great is the power, so great the majesty of the Lord; the secrets of darkness are detected by it's light; nor could hidden crimes be conceled from the Priest of God; for this happened to an infant, which was not yet of age to speak, or tell the crimes which others had committed upon it. There was another woman," says *Cyprian*, "who, after she had taken the sacrament with us unobserved, was instantly seized with pains and torments, and fell down convulsed and trembling, as if she had swallowed a sword or deadly poyson: and her crime, which had escaped the notice of men, met with it's punishment from God. Another, who had attempted with her polluted hands to open her chest, [in which, the consecrated elements, according to the custom of that age, were kept for her use at home,] fire burst out of it in such a manner that she durst not touch it. Another man, who had also been defiled, having had the assurance to take a part of the consecrated bread among the rest undiscovered, could neither eat nor handle it, but instead of it found a coal of fire in his hands."

Now what other notion can we reasonably entertain of these strange stories, but that they were partly forged, and partly aggravated and dressed up into this tragical form, from some accidental disorders, which the sense of a concealed guilt, and the dread of God's judgements upon it, would naturally raise in anxious minds, on that awfull occasion of receiving the Sacrament? For it is certain, that they were of the greatest use, in these times of danger and trial, to support the discipline of the Church, which the *Lord guarded*, as Mr. *Dodwell* says, *by these terrors, as by the sword of a Cherubim.* Since none of those, who had secretly lapsed, or been weak enough to deny the faith, and from a desire of conceling their shame, had evaded the penance of the Church, durst either come openly to the Sacrament, or take it even privately at home, or yet wholly abstain from it, when the divine judgements were so signally exerted upon all, who had ventured on any of those expedients, before they had made a public satisfaction for their crime, and been absolved of it in form by the Pastors of the Church. And it was without doubt for this end, that all these stories, with many more of the same kind, were so pompously and rhetorically set forth by this eminent Bishop, in his celebrated treatise concerning the *lapsed* Christians.

Sect. 5. As to the gift of *expounding the Scriptures, or the mysteries of God*, by a divine inspiration, which is clamed likewise by the Primitive Fathers, there is not the least trace of it to be found in any age of the Church, from the days of the Apostles. For in the second and third Centuries, the very period, in which all the other miraculous gifts are supposed to have flourished in their greatest vigor, it is certain, as we have seen above, that a most senseless, extravagant, and enthusiastic method of expounding prevailed, which has ever since been utterly slighted and rejected: whereas in these later days, when all extraordinary gifts are confessedly ceased, a clear, solid, and rational way of interpreting generally obtains, as the warmest advocates of Antiquity are forced to allow. And whenever any particular Father happens to be censured for his ridiculous comments on Sacred Writ, his Apologists with one voice alledge, that such expositions are not to be charged to the man, *but to the age in which he lived*, which could not relish or indure any better.

Justin Martyr however lays claim to this gift, as

conferred upon him by the special grace of God, upon which Mr. *Tillemont* declares, "that of all the extraordinary graces, which the Holy Spirit bestowed upon the Church in those times, there were few so considerable, as that of understanding the Scriptures, which was communicated by singular favor to *Justin.*" Yet from all the writings and monuments of the very earliest Fathers, which remain to us, it is manifest, beyond all contradiction, that there never was any such gift in the Church, after the times of the Apostles; and that *Justin* in particular, had no better claim to it, than any of the rest. And if those Fathers then, through a fervency of zeal, or an enthusiastic turn of mind, could mistake such fancifull expositions for divine inspirations, I see no reason why they might not as easily be deluded in every other instance of those pretended gifts, which flattered the same zeal and spirit, that so strongly possessed them.

It is a common case with men of great piety, zealously persuaded of the truth and high importance of any religious doctrine, to think it reasonable that God should interpose himself miraculously in favor of it, when it happens to be opposed by any earthly power and in danger of being oppressed: and when they are thus prepared by their prejudices, to expect a divine interposition, they listen to every pretension of that sort, which craft or wild enthusiasm can devise, without allowing their reason to examine it, or to suggest the suspicion of a fraud. There are many instances of this in History, and a remarkable one in our own; that of *the Holy Maid of Kent*, in the reign of *Henry the VIII.*: who by the pretence of *visions and divine revelations*, communicated in *trances or ecstacy*, contrived by Popish Priests, to raise the sinking credit of their cause, drew in Bishop *Fisher*, with many other eminent persons, to take her for a *Prophetess*, divinely inspired, as *Tertullian* did his *ecstatic Maid*. Yet this modern Prelate was more learned and judicious, than any one perhaps of all the ancient Fathers, and by all accounts of him, as pious and religious too: since he lost his life, or, in the stile of the *Romish* Church, suffered martyrdom, for the sake of those very prejudices, which betrayed him into this folly. But the Lord *Cromwell*, expostulating with him on that subject, rightly told him, "that the true reason, which induced him to give credit to the maid, was the matter of her prophecies; to which he was so addicted, that nothing could come amiss, which served to that end; and he appealed to his conscience, whether, if she had prophesied in favor of the King's proceedings, he would have given such easy credit to her, and not have examined the matter farther."

Sect. 6. The *gift of tongues* also is clamed, as we have seen, among the rest, and affirmed to have been actually possessed by the primitive Christians: for if the testimony of *Irenæus* can be credited, many were indued with it in his days, and heard *to speak all kinds of languages in the Church*. And in truth, this gift, in the common estimation of human reason, has been thought so essentially necessary to the propagation of the Gospel, in those first ages, that the advocates of the primitive miracles, trusting to that hypothesis, instead of searching into the fact, urge the necessity of it's continuance after the days of the Apostles, as a proof of the continuance of all the rest. Yet how great soever the importance of it may seem to be, it is evident, as I have elsewhere shewn, from the origin, nature and exercise of it, as they are represented in the New Testament, that it was not permanent or lasting, either in the Church at large, or in those particular persons, who were principally favored with it, but was granted onely on certain special occasions, and then again withdrawn, even from the Apostles themselves; so that, in the ordinary course of their ministry, they appear to have been generally destitute of it.

Irenæus however declares it to have been indulged to many in his days. But it is very remarkable, that this primitive Bishop, who ascribes it so liberally to others, appears to have been in great want of it himself, for the propagation of the Gospel in his own *Diocese*, among the *Celtæ*, or *Gauls*; where, as Dr. *Cave* interprets his words, *it was not the least part of his trouble, that he was forced to learn the language of the country, a rude and barbarous dialect, before he could do any good upon them.* Nor is it less strange also, that from the time of *Irenæus* there is not a single Father, in all the succeding ages, who, upon his authority, has ventured to carry on the same pretension, or make the least claim to it; or to speak of it in any other manner, than as a gift peculiar to the first Christians in the times of the Apostles. And I might risk the merit of my argument on this single point; that, after the apostolic times, there is not in all history one instance, either well attested, or even so much as mentioned, of any particular person who had ever exercised this gift, or pretended to exercise it, in any age or country whatsoever. Mr. *Dodwell* supposes it to have ceased in the reign of *M. Aurelius*, about sixty years after the death of St. *John*. But it is not credible that a gift of such eminent use should intirely cease, while all the rest were subsisting in full vigor, and abounding every day more and more. If, according to the common hypothesis, we admit them all to be true, it is not possible, I say, to imagine any cause why this in particular should be withdrawn, and the rest continued; but if, agreeably to my system, we consider them all as fictitious, we then see an obvious and manifest reason for it. For all the other extraordinary gifts, *of healing diseases, casting out devils, visions, and ecstatic revelations*, afford great room to impostors to exert all their craft of surprizing and dazzling the senses of the simple, the credulous, and the superstitious of all ranks; whereas the *gift of tongues* cannot easily be counterfeited, or a pretension to it imposed on men of sense, or on any indeed but those who are utterly illiterate and strangers to all tongues but their own: and to acquire a number of languages by natural means, and to a degree that might make them pass for a supernatural gift, was a work of so much difficulty and labor, as rendered it impracticable to support a pretension of that kind for a succession of many years. And this, in all probability, was the real cause of it's being dropped so early in those primitive ages: for after the mention of it by *Irenæus*, we find it no longer in any subsequent list of the miraculous gifts, nor the least hint of it's continuance in the Church in any later writer, from that time down to the present. If this then appears to have been the case of this particular gift; that a false claim to it was made by the early Fathers, and held up for a while till it could no longer be supported; it is sufficient, one would think, of itself, to blast the general credit of all the rest, tho' no particular mark of fraud could have been fixed on each of them separately: but when there is not a single one among them all, which, either from it's nature, or end, or manner of exertion, or the character of it's witnesses, does not furnish just ground to suspect it as fictitious, it must needs persuade every rational inquirer that they were all derived from the same source of craft and imposture.

In short, if we trace the history of this gift from its origin, we shall find, that in the times of the Gospel, in which alone the miracles of the Church are allowed to be true by all Christians, it was the first gift which was conferred upon the Apostles, in a public and illustrious manner, and reckoned ever after among the principal of those which were imparted to the first converts. But in the succeding ages, when miracles began to be of a suspected and dubious character, it is observable, that this gift is mentioned but once by a single writer, and then vanished of a sudden, without the least notice or hint given by any of the ancients, either of the manner, or time, or cause of it's vanishing. Lastly, in the later ages, when the miracles of the Church were not onely suspected, but found to be false by our Reformers, and considered as such ever since by all Protestants, this gift has never once been heard of, or pretended to by the Romanists themselves, tho' they challenge at the same time all the other gifts of the Apostolic days. From all which, I think, we may reasonably infer, that *the gift of tongues* may be considered as a proper test and criterion for determining the miraculous pretensions of all Churches which derive their descent from the Apostles; and consequently, if, in the list of their extraordinary gifts, they cannot shew us this, we may fairly conclude, that they have none else to shew which are real and genuin.

I have now run through all the various kinds of the miraculous gifts which are pretended to have subsisted in the Church during the second and third centuries, and have opened the genuin state of them, as far as it is discoverable to us at this distance, from the most authentic monuments and testimonies of the principal Fathers of those centuries. Ages, which are always stiled the purest, and in which these very Fathers bore the first character; not onely on the account of their piety and integrity, but of their abilities also and learning. If any suspicions then can be entertained against such witnesses, they will be stronger still against all who succeded them, especially after the Empire became Christian, when, according to the hypothesis of the very admirers of these primitive ages, a general corruption both of faith and morals began more openly to infect the Christian Church; which by that revolution, as St. *Jerom* says, *lost as much of her virtue as it had gained of power and wealth.*

But in the case of these miracles, there is one circumstance common to all the writers who attest them, as well as in the earlier as the later ages, that tho' their assertions be strong their instances are weak; and when, in proof of what they affirm, they descend to alledge any particular facts, they are usually so unlucky in the choice of them, that instead of strengthening, they weaken, the credit of their general affirmation, and, from the absurdity of each miracle related by them, furnish a fresh objection to their power of working any. This the reader can hardly fail to observe from the examples already produced; to which I shall add one or two more of the most considerable, which are transmitted to us from the same ages, and which I had before omitted to recite.

One of the most authentic and celebrated pieces in all primitive antiquity, is *the circular letter of the Church of Smyrna,* containing a narrative of the Martyrdom of St. *Polycarp,* their Bishop, and *of the many miracles,* as Mr. *Dodwell* says, *which made it illustrious.* This letter, written about the middle of the second century, informs us, "that when that Saint was entring the lists, in which he was to be burnt, there was so great a tumult that no body could be heard. But there came a voice to him from heaven, saying, *be strong,* Polycarp, *and acquit thyself like a man;* and tho' no body saw who it was that spake, yet many of the brethren heard the voice. As soon as he had finished his prayer, the executioner kindled the fire, and the flame began to blaze to a great height. When behold, says the writer, a mighty wonder appeared to us, whose lot it was to see it, and who were reserved by heaven to declare to others what we had seen. For the flame, forming a kind of arch, like to the sail of a ship filled with the wind, encompassed the body of the martyr as in a circle, who stood in the midst of it, not as flesh which is burnt, but bread which is baked, or as gold and silver glowing in a furnace; and so sweet a smell issued from him all the while, as if it had been the smoak of frankincense or some rich spices. At length, when these wicked men saw that his body could not be consumed by fire, they commanded the executioner to draw near, and to thrust his sword into him; which being done accordingly, there came out of his Body *a Dove*, and so great a quantity of blood as quite extinguished the fire; so that the whole multitude were amazed to see so great a difference between the unbelievers and the elect." Yet it appears from the sequel of the narrative, that there was fire enough still left to consume the body to ashes, which was executed with great care, that the Christians might not be able to preserve the least remains of it.

The greatest part of this Epistle is transcribed by *Eusebius*, who has omitted the mention of *the Dove* which flew out of his body; for which reason Mr. *Dodwell and Archbishop Wake* have thought fit also to omit it. Yet all the oldest copies still extant, from which *Archbishop Usher*, *Cotelerius*, and *Ruinart*, published their several editions, retain this passage; which *Eusebius* might probably drop for the same reason for which Mr. *Dodwell* and Bishop *Wake* also profess to have dropt it; viz., for the sake of rendring the narrative *the less suspected*. To the end of this letter is annexed the following advertisement. "This Epistle was transcribed by *Caius* from the copy of *Irenæus*, the disciple of *Polycarp;* and I, *Socrates*, transcribed it at *Corinth*. After which, I, *Pionius*, again wrote it out from the copy above mentioned, having searched it out by the revelation of *Polycarp*, who directed me to it," &c.

Eusebius also relates a miracle wrought by *Narcissus*, Bishop of *Jerusalem*, about the end of the second or the beginning of the third century; "that when the sacred oil was almost spent, in the vigil of *Easter*, and the people were in a great consternation about it, he ordered those, who had the care of the lamps, to go and draw water from a certain well in the neighbourhood, and to bring it away to him; which being accordingly done, *Narcissus*, after he had prayed over it, commanded them to pour it into the lamps with a sincere faith in Christ; upon which, by a miraculous and divine power, the nature of the water was changed into the fatness of oil; of which oil, as *Eusebius* says, several small quantities were preserved by great numbers of the faithfull, to his time, which was about an hundred years after the date of the miracle."

The same Historian, giving an account of the horrible barbarities which were exercised upon the Christians of *Palæstine*, concludes one of his stories in the following manner: "after these things had been transacted many days successively, this miracle appeared. There was a clear and bright sky, and a remarkable screnity of the air; when on a sudden, the pillars in the portico's of the City, poured out drops of tears; and when there was not the least moisture in the air, the streets and public places were all wet, no body knew how, as if water had been thrown upon them; so that it became a common talk, that the earth wept for the impiety which was committed, and to reprove the relentless and savage nature of men, stones and inanimate bodies shed tears for what had happened." A description of this kind might easily be excused in an Orator or a Poet, but when an Historian, after he has raised our attention and prepared us to expect something great and miraculous, tells us onely *of stones shedding tears for the impieties of men,* he debases the gravity of History, and makes miracles themselves contemptible.

Mr. *Dodwell,* as I have before said, has, with great diligence, deduced the History of the primitive miracles down to these very times of *Eusebius,* which he then shuts up with the establishment of Christianity by human laws, declaring, "that many things concurred to recommend the credit of the preceding ages, which have no place in those that followed:" and speaking of the Life of *Gregory,* called the *wonder-worker,* written by *Gregory of Nyssa,* a Bishop of the greatest piety and gravity, he says "in this Life there are many things which breath the air of imposture and the genius of the fourth century, so that I dare not mix them with what is more genuin, for fear of hurting the credit of all." For this reason therefore, it was my first intention, to confine my inquiries also to the same period; but having since perceived, that several of our learned Divines and principal advocates of the Christian faith have not scrupled to assert the succession of true miracles to the end even of the fifth century, I thought it necessary to extend my argument to the same length, lest I should seem to neglect any evidence which could be offered to me, and especially such as is declared to be *convincing* and *decisive* by men of their character. But from every step that we advance forward, we shall readily perceive, that Mr. *Dodwell*, who had as much piety and more learning than any of them, has in this respect shewn more judgement too, by restraining the miraculous powers of the Church to the three first centuries.

In the fourth century, we find some of the principal Fathers delivering themselves on this subject so variously and inconsistently, as shews, that tho' they were ashamed to deny what they knew to be true, yet they were desirous to inculcate what they knew to be false. For on some occasions, when they are pressed, they plainly confess that miracles were then ceased; yet on others, they appeal to them again as common, and performed among them every day. For example, St. *Chrysostom* observes, "that in the infancy of the Church, the extraordinary gifts of the spirit were bestowed even on the unworthy, because those early times stood in need of that help for the more easy propagation of the Gospel; but now, says he, they are not given even to the worthy, because the present strength of the Christian faith is no longer in want of them." In another place, speaking of the miraculous powers of the Apostles, and of the force which they had in converting the Gentile world, "wherefore," adds he, "because no miracles are wrought now, we are not to take it for a proof that none were wrought then; for then they were of use, but now they are not; for the first planters of the Gospel were simple and ignorant men, and had nothing to teach from themselves, but what they received from God, that they delivered to the world; so we likewise of these times, bring nothing indeed of our own, but what we received from them, that we declare to all. Nor do we yet persuade by the force of our reason, but evince the truth of our doctrines from the Holy Scriptures and the miracles then wrought in confirmation of them." Again, speaking of the Jews, in our Saviour's time, who *desired a sign,* he says, "there are some also even now, who desire and ask why are not miracles performed still at this day? and why are there no persons who raised the dead and cure diseases?" To which he replies, "that it was owing to the want of faith and virtue and piety in those times." On another occasion also he declares, "that St. *Paul's* Handkerchiefs could once do greater miracles than all the Christians of his days could do with ten thousand prayers and tears." Lastly, in *his books of consolation,* addressed to his friend *Stagirius,* who was supposed to be possessed and horribly tormented by an evil spirit, it is expressly signified, "that neither the tombs of the Martyrs, to which he had often applied for relief, nor the repeated endeavours of the most holy and celebrated Exorcists of those days, were able to drive the Devil out of him."

There are several other passages in this Father of the same strain; in which he allows the cessation of miracles, and speaks of them even with contempt, "as proper onely to rouse the dull and sluggish, but useless to men of philosophical minds; that they were frequently liable to sinister suspicions, of being mere phantasms and illusions, and that it was a proof of the greater generosity of that age, to take God's word without such pledges."

From these testimonies, one would necessarily conclude, upon the authority of St. *Chrysostom*, that miracles were ceased in his days: yet in other parts of his works we find him in a different story, and haranguing on the mighty wonders, which were performed among them every day, *by the reliques of the Martyrs, in casting out Devils, curing all diseases, and drawing whole Cities and people to their Sepulchers.* He displays also the miraculous cures wrought by the use *of consecrated oil, and by the sign of the Cross;* which last he calls *a defence against all evil, and a medicine against all sickness, and affirms it to have been miraculously impressed, in his own time, on people's garments.*

St. *Austin* also, who lived at the same time, tho' in a different part of the world, takes notice of the same objection, made by the Sceptics, with which the Christians were commonly urged in this age. "They ask us, says he, *why are not those miracles performed now, which you declare to have been wrought formerly?* I could tell them, that they were then necessary, before the world believed, for this very purpose, that the world might believe; but he, who still requires prodigies, that he may become a believer, is himself a great prodigy, who does not believe now, when the world does believe." One would not imagine, that these words, which seem to imply a cessation of miracles, were the preface to an elaborate narrative and solemn attestation of great numbers of them, said to have been wrought in these very times: which, if true, as they are here affirmed by St. *Austin* from his own knowledge, must have been more illustrious, both for the number and the excellence of them, than all which were wrought by the Apostles themselves.

But before we descend to particulars, I cannot forbear observing, what this Father has delivered concerning the general state and credit of them among the Christians themselves, at the very time when they were wrought. He tells us then, that tho' miracles were frequently wrought, either by the *name of Jesus, or by his Sacraments, or by the prayers or the memorials of the Martyrs;* yet the fame of them was not so illustrious as of those of the Apostles, since they were scarce ever known to the whole City or place where they happened to be performed, but for the most part to a very few onely; while all the rest were utterly ignorant of them; especially if the city was large: and if ever they were told abroad to other people, yet they were not recommended with such authority, as to be received without difficulty and doubting, tho' reported by true believers to true believers."

That he might put an end therefore to this strange negligence of the Christians, with regard to their own miracles, he took care, as oft as he heard of any miracle, "that the parties concerned in it should be examined, and a verbal proces, or authentic narrative be drawn of the fact, which was afterwards publicly read to the people. Yet all this caution, as he says, was not sufficient to make the miracles known, or at all regarded: because those who were present at the recital of such narratives heard them but once, while the greater part were absent; and even those who heard them, retained nothing a few days after of what they had heard, and seldom or never took the pains to tell it to any body else whom they knew to be absent." This account of the matter would be very surprizing, were it not explained to us by the miracles themselves, of which I have here added a few specimens, whence we shall easily collect the reason of that coldness and indifference, which the people of those days expressed towards them.

For instance, among many other stories of the same kind, he relates these, which follow: "A pious old Cobler of *Hippo*, where he himself was Bishop, having lost his old coat, and wanting money to buy a new one, betook himself to *the twenty Martyrs*, whose chappel or memorial was famous in that city; where he prayed to them very earnestly, that he might be enabled by them to get some cloaths. Some young Fellows, who overheard him, began to make sport with him, and pursued him with their scoffs, for begging money to buy a coat. But as the old man walked away, without minding them, he saw a large fish lie gasping on the shore, which he caught by the help of the young men, and sold to a Christian Cook, for three hundred peace; and laying out the money on wooll, set his wife to work, to provide cloaths for him: but the Cook, cutting open the fish, found a gold ring also in the belly of it; which out of compassion to the poor man, and the terror also of religion, he presently carried to the Cobler, saying, *see here is the cloathing, which the twenty Martyrs have given you.*

There was one *Hesperius* likewise, as he tells us, a man of Tribunician quality, whose country house near *Hippo* was haunted by evil spirits, and his cattel also and servants afflicted by them: upon which he sent a message to the Priests at *Hippo*, when *Austin* happened to be absent, that some of them would come over to him, and drive the evil Spirits away by their prayers. One of them accordingly went, and offered *the sacrifice of Christ's body* upon the spot, praying at the same time, as fervently as he was able, that this vexation might be removed; upon which by God's mercy it instantly ceased.

"The same *Hesperius* had received from a friend some *holy earth,* brought from *Jerusalem,* where Christ rose from his grave on the third day; which earth he hung up in his bedchamber, to secure himself from the mischief of those evil spirits. But since his house was now cleared of them, he was considering, what he should do with this earth, being unwilling, out of reverence to it, to keep it any longer in his bedchamber. It happened, that St. *Austin* and another Bishop, called *Maximinus*, were then in the neighbourhood; so that *Hesperius* sent them an invitation to come to his house; which they immediately accepted; and after he had acquainted them with the whole affair, he desired, that *the sacred earth* might be deposited somewhere in the ground, and an Oratory built over it, where the Christians might assemble for the performance of divine service: the two Bishops had no objection, so that his project was presently executed. There was at the same place a country lad, afflicted with the palsy; who having heard what was done, begged of his parents, that they would carry him without delay to that holy place: whither as soon as he was brought, he put up his prayers, and presently returned back on foot in perfect health."

There are many more tales of this sort, as contemptible as any in the Popish legends, and all attested by this celebrated Father, from his own knowledge: yet these are nothing to the extravagant things which he goes on to relate of *the reliques of the Martyr Stephen.* For as *reliques* were now become the most precious treasure of the Church, so these of St. *Stephen,* after they had lain buried and unknown for near four centuries, were reveled in a vision to one *Lucianus,* a Priest, *by* Gamaliel, *the celebrated Doctor of the Law, at whose feet St. Paul had been bred,* and being found by his direction, were removed with great solemnity and many miracles into *Jerusalem.* The fame of these reliques was soon spread through the Christian world; and many little portions of them brought away by holy Pilgrims, to enrich the particular Churches of their own countries. For wherever any reliques were deposited, an Oratory or Chappel was always built over them, which was called a Memorial of that Martyr whose reliques it contained. Several reliques therefore of St. *Stephen* having been brought by different people into *Afric*, as many Memorials of him were consequently erected in different places, of which three were peculiarly famous: one at *Hippo*, where St. *Austin* was Bishop; a second at *Calama*, and a third at *Uzalis*, two other Episcopal Cities; and many great and illustrious miracles were continually wrought in them all.

St. *Austin* has given us a particular relation of some of them, by which *the gout, the stone, and fistulas* were instantly cured; *the blind restored to sight; and five different persons raised even from death to life.* Two of whom were carried dead to the reliques, and brought back alive; two more restored to life, by the virtue of their garments onely, which had touched the reliques; and a fifth, by the oil of the Martyr's lamps. After all which wonderfull stories, he adds the following apology, not for telling us so many of them, but so few, out of the infinite number which were publicly known and recorded.

"What shall I do?" says he; "I am engaged by promise to finish the present work, so that it is not possible for me in this place to relate all the miracles which I know; and our people without doubt, when they read these, will be grieved that I have omitted so many, which they know to be true as well as I.

But I beg them to excuse me, and to consider what a tedious piece of work it would be, to do that, which the nature of my argument does not oblige me to do here. For were I to relate onely the miracles of cures, without mentioning the rest which have been performed by this Martyr, the most glorious *Stephen*, in the colony of *Calama*, and in our own, it would fill a great number of volumes. Nor would it be possible to collect them all, but such of them onely of which certificates have been made and read to the people. For this I ordered to be done, when I saw the effects of the divine powers, like to those of the ancients, so frequently exerted also in our own times, which ought not to be lost from the notice of the multitude. It is not yet two years since this Memorial was founded at *Hippo*, and tho' I am certain that no account was taken of many of the miracles, yet at the time when I wrote this, the number of certificates publicly made amounted to near seventy: but at *Calama*, where the Memorial is of longer standing, and certificates more frequently taken, they reach to a far greater number.

"At *Uzalis* also, we know many eminent miracles wrought by the same Martyr; whose Memorial was instituted there by their Bishop *Evodius*, much earlier than with us. But it is not the custom with them to take certificates, or it was not rather, because now it is probably begun. For when I was lately there, I exhorted *Petronia*, a celebrated Matron, who had been miraculously cured of a great and lingering illness, in which the physicians were not able to help her, to get a certificate drawn of the case, and read publicly to the people; to which, by the advice also of the said Bishop of the place, she willingly consented, and inserted in it another miracle, which, notwithstanding the hast that I am in to put an end to this work, I cannot forbear relating, &c."

I have dwelt the longer on these miracles than the importance of them perhaps may be thought to require; but they are so precisely described and authentically attested by one of the most venerable Fathers in all antiquity, who affirms them to have been wrought within his own knowledge, and under his own eyes, that they seem of all others the best adapted to evince the truth of what I have been advancing, and to illustrate the real character of all the other miracles of the primitive times, both before and after them. Dr. *Chapman*, however, speaking of the very same miracles, roundly declares them all *to be so strongly attested, both by the effects and the relators of them, that to doubt their reality, were to doubt the evidence of sense.* On these then I am content to rest the fate of my whole argument; and if either Dr. *Chapman* or Dr. *Berriman* can maintain these miracles to be credible, shall no longer dispute the credibility of any, from the apostolic times down to our own. But, on the other hand, if miracles so strictly examined by a most holy Bishop, confirmed by the certificates of eye-witnesses, and rehearsed publicly to the people, at the time when they are said to have been wrought cannot command our belief, these doctors must needs confess, nay, they have already confessed, that the Christian Church can shew no other, except those of Christ and his Apostles, which can make any better pretensions to it.

For not to insist on the objections which might reasonably be made to the probability of the facts themselves; to the incompetency of the instruments by which, and of the ends for which, they are said to have been performed; to the credulity of a prejudiced, or the fidelity rather of an artfull and interested relator; it seems evident, from the neglect with which they were treated by the Christians themselves; from the obscurity in which they lay; from the diligence of St. *Austin* to search them out; to get certificates of them, and to publish them to the people; and from the insufficiency of all his pains to make them still regarded or at all remembered; that the people themselves saw or suspected the cheat, and were tired with the repeated frauds of this kind which their Bishops were imposing upon them. For it is not possible to conceive any other reason of so surprizing a coldness, in a case of all others the most warming, but a general persuasion, grounded on experience, that these pretended miracles were nothing else but forgeries, contrived to enforce some favorite doctrine or rite, which the rulers of the Church were desirous to establish.

Yet these are not the stories which chiefly shock Mr. *Dodwell*, and oblige him to reject the miracles of the fourth century; but others still more extravagant, tho' attested likewise by persons of equal eminence and authority; by St. *Athanasius*, St. *Gregory* of *Nyssa*, St. *Jerom*, St. *Epiphanius*, &c. Of which, therefore, it will be necessary to add a specimen or two from each of those Fathers.

St. *Athanasius*, in the Preface to his Life of St. *Antony* the Monk, declares, "that he had inserted nothing in it, but what he either knew to be true, having often seen the saint himself, or what he had learnt from one who had long ministered to him, and poured water upon his hands." In this life then, after a great number of monstrous stories concerning the personal conflicts which this Saint continually sustained with all the several Devils and powers of hell, who assaulted him in every shape which could imprint terror, and exerted every art and even corporal punishments to drive him from the monastic life, which threatened the speedy ruin of their kingdom, he tells us; "that somebody knocking one day at his cell, *Antony* went to the door, where he saw a tall meagre person, who being asked his name, answered, *that he was Satan*. His business, it seems, was to beg a truce of the Saint, and to expostulate with him on account of the perpetual reproaches and curses which the Monks so undeservedly bestowed upon him, when he was no longer in condition to give them any trouble: for since the desert was now filled with Monks, and the Christians spread into all places, he was disarmed of all power to do them any mischief: so that the Christians had nothing more to do but to take care of themselves, and to forbear their needless curses against him." The rest of this piece is filled with many other miracles of the same stamp, too trifling to deserve any regard.

St. *Gregory* of *Nyssa*, in the life of his namesake, called the wonder-worker, has this story; "that the *Virgin Mary*, accompanied by St. *John* the Evangelist, appeared to *Gregory* in a vision, and explained to him the mystery of Godliness, in a short creed or divine summary of faith, which he took down in writing as they dictated it to him, and left the copy of it a legacy to the Church of *Neocæsarea*, of which he was Bishop: and if any one, says he, has a mind to be satisfied of the truth of this, let him inquire of that Church, in which the very words, as they were written by his blessed hand, are preserved to this day: which, for the excellency of the divine grace, may be compared with those tables of the law made by God and delivered to *Moses*."

Dr. *Waterland* has given us a translation of this creed, and Dr. *Berriman*, an abstract of it; which is *as express as possible*, they say, *for the doctrine of the Trinity, as it was taught afterwards by* Athanasius. They both however intimate, that the genuineness of the creed had been called in quæstion, tho' without any sufficient cause. Yet the learned *Cave*, who for zeal and orthodoxy, and facility of believing, was scarce inferior to any, declares, *that notwithstanding the authority of* Gregory Nyssen, *who was apt to be too credulous, this short exposition of the Christian faith will hardly find credit with prudent and sensible men.* But whatever may be alledged to persuade us, that this creed was actually professed and taught by *Gregory*, in his Church of *Neocæsarea*, yet no man surely but Dr. *Berriman* could have any scruple to own, that the story of the vision, and of it's delivery to him from heaven, was a forgery, contrived to support the *Athanasian doctrine,* at a time when it was warmly controverted, and in danger of being suppressed. But as the revelation of it, if admitted to be true, would put an end at once to all dispute, and give a divine sanction to the doctrine itself, so the doctor seems resolved not to part with it: for in his *Historical Account of the Trinitarian Controversy,* speaking on this very point, he says; "there are many arguments to convince us of the genuineness and authority of this Creed of St. *Gregory;* I do not mean of it's being taught him by revelation, *(tho' that may be well attested too, and will not seem incredible to those who shall consider how highly this great person was distinguished by the charismata, or extraordinary gifts of the Holy Ghost,)* but I mean, as to the certainty of it's having been taught by St. *Gregory,"* &c. From which we see, that tho' his sole business in this place was to prove the creed to have been really *Gregory's,* yet he could not forbear to acquaint us, that, if there was occasion, he could prove *the revelation* also to be genuin: since it cannot enter into his head how any one should think it incredible, that in those miraculous ages a person of *Gregory's* exalted character might be favored with a visit from heaven, by the *Virgin Mary* and *St. John the Apostle.*

The same *Gregory of Nyssa* relates likewise, " how his namesake, being upon a journey, was forced one night to take shelter in an heathen temple, famed for an oracle and divination; where the Dæmons used to appear visibly and offer themselves to the priests. But the holy Father, by invoking the name of *Jesus*, put them all to flight; and by making the sign of the cross, purified the air, polluted by the steam of their sacrifices. The next morning, when the Priest came to perform his usual functions, the Devils appeared, and acquainted him that they had been driven out the night before by a stranger, and had not the power to return: nor was he able to recall them by all the charms of his expiatory sacrifices. Upon this, the Priest pursued *Gregory* in great wrath, and overtaking him on the road, threatened him most terribly for what he had done. But *Gregory*, despising his threats, gave him to understand that he had a power superior to that of Devils, and could drive them whithersoever he pleased. The Priest, amazed at what he said, began to beg, that for a proof of his power he would fetch them back again into the temple; to which *Gregory* consenting, wrote this short note onely upon a schedule of paper, *Gregory to Satan. Enter.* With this, the Priest was dismissed; and laying the little schedule upon the altar, brought the Devils back again immediately to their old seats." The miracle however had the good effect of converting the Pagan Priest.

I have already given a passage from the Life of St. *Hilarion* the Monk, written by St. *Jerom*, as a specimen of the fidelity of the writer. But for a proof of the fabulous genius of the fourth century, Mr. *Dodwell* refers us to another Life of *the Hermit Paul*, compiled by the same Father, which is filled with stories still more monstrous; "of *Satyrs and Fauns* presenting themselves to the Hermit, and confessing their own mortality, and the folly of the Gentiles in paying them any worship, and begging his recommendation of them to their common Lord, who came to save the world; of a raven bringing half a loaf for sixty years successively to the Hermit, for his dayly food in the wilderness; and then a whole loaf, when St. *Antony* came to visit him: of two lions coming to assist *Antony* in the burial of *Paul*, by digging a grave for him with their feet, and then departing with the blessing of *Antony*."

St. *Epiphanius*, Bishop of *Salamis* in *Cyprus*, who is said to have wrought miracles himself, both in his life-time and after it, affirms several false and absurd miracles from his own knowledge, which his advocates gently pass over by remarking onely, that *this most holy Father was too credulous*, or *not so accurate*, as we could wish. He declares, "that in imitation of our Saviour's miracle at *Cana* in *Galilee*, several fountains and rivers in his days were annually turned into wine. A fountain of *Cibyra*, a City of *Caria*, says he, and another at *Gerasa* in *Arabia*, prove the truth of this. I myself have drunk out of the fountain of *Cibyra*, and my brethren, out of the other at *Gerasa;* and many testify the same thing of the river *Nile* in *Ægypt*." Should we then be asked here, as we were before in a similar case, *will ye not believe a most holy Bishop, in a fact attested by his own senses?* the answer is clear and short, *the fact is not credible.*

St. *Chrysostom*, celebrating the acts of the Martyr St. *Babylas*, Bishop of *Antioch*, says, "the Gentiles will laugh to hear me talk of the acts of persons dead and buried, and consumed to dust; but they are not to imagine, that the bodies of Martyrs, like to those of common men, are left destitute of all active force and energy, since a greater power than that of the human soul is superadded to them, the power of the Holy Spirit; which, by working miracles in them, demonstrates the truth of the resurrection." He then procedes to inform us, "how the remains of this Martyr were removed by a certain Emperor, out of the City of *Antioch,* into a suburb of it, called *Daphne,* famous for the delights of it's situation, and the variety of pleasures which it afforded to it's inhabitants, as well as for a celebrated Temple and *Oracle of Apollo Daphneus;* to which the body of the Saint was thought proper to be removed, for the sake of giving some check to the lewdness and licentiousness that reigned in the place. The coffin therefore was no sooner deposited in a chappel provided for it, than the Oracle of *Apollo* was struck dumb at once; so that when *Julian* the Apostate came afterwards to consult it, he could receive no other answer from *Apollo, but that the dead would not suffer him to speak any longer.* Wherefore *Julian* commanded the bones of St. *Babylas* to be conveyed back again into *Antioch;* but in the very moment when they entered into the City, the Statue of the God and the roof of his Temple were destroyed by lightning, upon the intercession of the Saint." St. *Chrysostom* employs an intire Homily, and a larger discourse, which follows it, in haranguing on this same subject of *Babylas,* and on the blessings and dayly miracles wrought by the reliques of the Martyrs to the edification of the Church and the confusion of unbelievers. Yet his History of this Saint is so evidently fabulous and romantic, that the *Benedictin Monks*, who published the last and best edition of his works, found it necessary to admonish the reader, *that it is written in a declamatory stile, overflowing with rhetorical figures, and for the most part destitute of truth.* In which those learned Papists have shewn more candor as well as judgement than our Protestant Doctor *Cave;* who, in his Life of the same *Babylas*, after relating the particular story just described, which he calls *one of the most memorable occurrences that Church antiquity has conveyed to us*, adds the following attestation to it.

"The reader 'tis like may be apt to scruple this story, as savouring a little of superstition, and giving too much honor to the reliques of saints. To which I shall say no more than that the credit of it seems unquæstionable; it being reported not onely by *Socrates*, *Sozomen*, and *Theodoret*, who all lived very near that time, but by *Chrysostom*, who was born at *Antioch*, and was a long time Presbyter of that Church, and was scholar there to *Libanius* the Sophist at the very time when the thing was done, and an eye-witness of it; and who not onely preached the thing, but wrote a discourse against the Gentiles on this very subject, where he appeals to the knowledge both of young and old then alive, who had seen it, and challenges them to stand up and contradict, if they could, the truth of what he had related. Nay, which farther puts the case past all peradventure, *Libanius* the Orator evidently confesses it," &c. Whereas all which that Orator confesses, and which the Benedictins allow to be well grounded in the whole relation, is, that the reliques of *Babylas* were carried back again, by *Julian's* order, out of *Daphne* into the City, and that the Temple of the *Daphnean Apollo* was soon after destroyed in the night by fire; which the Christians declared to have been sent from heaven by the power of the Saint, and the Heathens ascribed to the revenge and contrivance of the Christians.

A Popish writer, with whom I have been engaged, in order to reprove my raillery on their fictitious saints and image-worship, has alledged also a most notable miracle, from this fourth century; which I shall here add to the specimens already given.

"When *Julian the Apostate* was pursuing his *Persian* expedition, and at the very time when he is supposed to have been destroyed by the immediate hand of God, the Great St. *Basil* was standing before the *Image of the Blessed Virgin*, on which there was painted likewise the figure of St. *Mercurius*, an eminent Martyr: and while St. *Basil* was fervently praying that the impious and atheistical *Julian* might be cut off, he received this revelation from the picture; out of which the figure of the Martyr quite vanished for a little while, but presently appeared again and held out *a bloody spear*, as a token of what had happened in the same moment to *Julian*."

But *Julian's* death was foretold likewise by *visions* and *divine revelations*, as the Ecclesiastical writers inform us, to several other Saints and holy men, in different parts of the world, who were severally addressing their prayers to God for his destruction. Whence we cannot but observe, what a total change there was, both of principles and practice, between the Fathers of the fourth and those of the preceding ages; or between the Church when persecuted, and when established in power and authority. For in the earlier times, under the very worst of the Heathen Emperors and the cruellest persecutors of the Church, when the Christians were treated every where, as traitors to the government, all their Apologists, through the three first centuries, declare with one voice, that they were obliged by the precepts of their religion to be of all men the most loyal to their Princes, and that it was their dayly practice to put up their united prayers for their prosperity. We pray, says *Tertullian, for every Emperor, that he may have a long life, secure reign, a safe house, strong armies, faithfull Senate, honest people, a quiet world, and whatsoever else, man, or Cæsar himself can wish.* Yet after the Church had gained a firm establishment, it's temper was quite altered, and the Emperors no sooner began to give them any disturbance than their prayers were turned into curses, and the divine vengeance confessedly implored to destroy them. So true it is, what all the Popish writers have not scrupled to affirm, from *Pope Gregory the Great* down to *Cardinal Bellarmine, that it was not the want of will but of the power onely to rebel, which made the primitive Christians so patient under the persecuting Emperors, and particularly under Julian, because the Church had not yet acquired strength enough to controul the Princes of the earth.*

Now it is agreed by all, that these Fathers whose testimonies I have just been reciting, were the most eminent lights of the fourth Century; all of them sainted by the Catholic Church, and highly reverenced at this day in all Churches, for their piety, probity, and learning: yet from the specimens of them above given, it is evident that they would not scruple to propagate any fiction, how gross soever, which served to promote the interest either of Christianity in general, or of any particular rite or doctrine which they were desirous to recommend. St. *Jerom* in effect confesses it; for after the mention of a silly story, concerning the Christians of *Jerusalem*, who used to shew, in the ruins of the Temple, *certain stones of a reddish color*, which they pretended to have been stained by the blood of *Zacharias the Son of Barachias, who was slain between the Temple and the Altar*, he adds, *but I do not find fault with an error, which flows from an hatred of the Jews and a pious zeal for the Christian faith.*

If the miracles then of the fourth century, so solemnly attested by the most celebrated and revered Fathers of the Church, are to be rejected after all as fabulous, it must needs give a fatal blow to the credit of all the miracles even of the preceding centuries; since there is not a single Father whom I have mentioned in this fourth age, who for zeal and piety, may not be compared with the best of the more ancient, and for knowledge and learning be preferred to them all. For instance, there was not a person in all the primitive Church, more highly respected in his own days, than St. *Epiphanius*, for the purity of his life, as well as the extent of his learning. He was a Master of *five languages*, and has left behind him one of the most usefull works, which remain to us from antiquity. St. *Jerom*, who personally knew him, calls him, *the Father of all Bishops, and a shining Star among them; the pattern of ancient sanctity; the man of God of blessed memory; to whom the people used to flock in crouds, offering their little children to his benediction; kissing his feet; and catching the hem of his garment.*

All the rest were men of the same character, who spent their lives and studies in propagating the faith, and in combating the vices and heresies of their times. Yet none of them have scrupled, we see, to pledge their faith for the truth of facts which no man of sense can believe, and which their warmest admirers are forced to give up as fabulous. If such persons then could willfully attempt to deceive; and if the sanctity of their characters cannot assure us of their fidelity; what better security can we have from those, who lived before them? or what cure for our Scepticism with regard to any of the miracles above mentioned? Was the first Assertor of them, *Justin Martyr*, more pious, cautious, learned, judicious, or less credulous than *Epiphanius*? or were those virtues more conspicuous in *Irenæus, Tertullian, Cyprian, Arnobius*, and *Lactantius*, than in *Athanasius, Gregory, Chrysostom, Jerom, Austin*? No body, I dare say, will venture to affirm it. If these later Fathers then, biassed by a false zeal or interest, could be tempted to propagate a known lie; or with all their learning and knowledge, could be so weakly credulous, as to believe the absurd stories, which they themselves attest; there must always be reason to suspect, that the same prejudices would operate even more strongly in the earlier Fathers; prompted by the same zeal and the same interests, yet indued with less learning, less judgement, and more credulity.

But whatever light the fourth Century may give us, in discovering the real character of the earlier ages, it affords us at least a sure presage, of what we are to expect from the fifth, into which we are now entering. Dr. *Waterland* himself allows, on the authority of *Nazianzen, that the state of the Church towards the end of the fourth century was become very corrupt:* for that reason, as we have elsewhere seen, he durst not venture to appeal, in the case of it's miracles, to any of the celebrated Fathers above mentioned, as being evidently infected with that corruption. The learned *Mosheim* also, a foreign Divine, and zealous advocate of Christianity, who, by his writings against the Freethinkers, as Dr. *Chapman* tells us, *has deserved the esteem of all good and learned men,* intimates his fears, "that those, who search with any attention into the writings of the greatest and most holy Doctors of the fourth century, will find them all without exception, disposed *to deceive and to lie,* whenever the interest of religion requires it." Since the degeneracy therefore of this age has obliged the most devoted admirers of antiquity, not onely to suspect but to reject it's miracles as spurious, we cannot be at a loss what judgement we ought to form on the miracles of the following age, which is allowed by all to have been still more corrupt.

The succeding Fathers, however, go on still as before, to assert the same miraculous gifts, and even more of them to the fifth than to any of the preceding ages. Whence a certain infidel writer has taken occasion to censure the credit of Ecclesiastical History as being *full of miracles, wrought by such madmen as* Symeon Stylites, a Monk of the fifth century, who spent the greatest part of his life on the top of a pillar, from which he drew his surname; and whose wonderfull acts are particularly related by *Theodoret*. Now whether this *Symeon* was a madman or not, the credit of Christianity is no way affected by it. The History of the Gospel, I hope may be true, though the History of the Church be fabulous. And if the ecclesiastic Historians have recorded many silly fictions under the name of miracles, as they undoubtedly have, the blame must be charged to the writers, not to their religion. But the censure came from an Infidel, and for that reason, was at all events to be confuted; since to allow a grain of truth to one of that class, is to betray the cause of Christianity and to strengthen the hands of it's enemies.

This is the principle which generally animates the zeal, and glares through the writings of the modern advocates of our religion; and which in reality has done more hurt and discredit to it than all the attacks of it's open adversaries: and it was the same principle without doubt that gave birth to the defence of *Symeon Stylites,* which Dr. *Chap-*

man, in his remarks on the Author referred to, has thought fit to attempt in the following words:

"I know our Author too well to take his judgement either of madness or sense. 'Tis more than probable, that it is madness with him to believe any miracles at all, of any person, or at any time. So that we are not to wonder if *Symeon* and his miracles have no sort of credit with him. For this reason I address myself here, not to him, but to those who distinguish between truth and imposture, between clear and indisputable evidence, and that which is dark and suspicious. The great *Theodoret*, whose character for sense, learning, and piety, is abundantly known and confessed, was himself contemporary with *Symeon Stylites*, was personally and intimately acquainted with him, conversed with him for many years together, and declares himself an eye-witness to the wonderfull things related of him. He has given us an account of a great part of his Life, which he wrote while *Symeon* was yet alive, and appeals to all the world for the truth of what he says of him. He farther tells us that *Symeon* by his miracles converted many thousands of Pagans, especially the *Ishmaelites* or *Saracens*, to the Christian religion; that he himself, at *Symeon's* desire, gave many of them the Sacerdotal benediction, and was in manifest danger of losing his life by the impatience and eagerness of the Barbarians to receive it from him. If we may not admit such evidence as this in proof of a matter of fact, I am afraid we must shake the evidence of all human testimony, and believe nothing but what we see, and feel, and know ourselves. Nay farther, our Author cannot prove that there ever existed such a man as *Symeon Stylites*, by better evidence than that which I have produced to prove his miracles."

Here we see what a sort of character and language is prepared for those who dare to reject the miracles of *Symeon*. They must be men who *know not how to distinguish between truth and imposture; between indisputable and suspicious evidence; who shake the credit of all human testimony, and believe nothing but what they see themselves.* And all this assurance is grounded on the single testimony of *Theodoret*, to whom, in order to enhance his authority, he has added, according to his usual way, the title of *the Great*. But as the Doctor has carried his defence of monks and their miracles much farther than any other protestant, I believe, would venture to do, so it was natural to suspect that he had been drawn into it by some popish writer, of whom he had conceived a favorable opinion, and we find accordingly, that he has borrowed, not onely his notions, but his very expressions, from Mons. *Tillemont*, who talks in the same pompous strain of *Le Grand Theodoret, whose evidence cannot be slighted, he says, without shaking the credit of all human testimony*.

But let him borrow them from whomsoever he pleases; my business is, to inquire onely whether what he has borrowed and so peremptorily affirmed be true, or credible, or fit for a protestant divine to impose upon the consciences of Christians. This therefore is the point which I shall now procede to consider, from the authority of those very testimonies to which he himself has referred us.

We are told then by *Theodoret*, "that this *Symeon* spent the first part of his life in certain monasteries near *Antioch*, in *Syria*, mortifying his body by horrible austeries, not onely beyond the rules of their ordinary discipline, but above the force even of nature itself; till for his perseverance in these extravagancies, contrary to the admonitions of his rulers, he was turned out of the society, as giving an example that might be dangerous or fatal to those who attempted to imitate it. Upon this he retired to a separate cave or hut, where he took a fancy, after the example of *Moses* and *Elias*, to keep a fast and total abstinence from food for forty intire days. But when another holy man, called *Bassus*, represented to him the danger and even sin of an attempt which would probably destroy him, he complied so far as to suffer ten loaves and a pitcher of water to be immured with him in his cell, with a promise to make use of them if he happened to want any refreshment. *Bassus* then closed up his door with mud, and left him for forty days; at the end of which he returned, and clearing away the mud from the door, found the ten loaves intire, and the pitcher also full, but *Symeon* stretched upon the ground, quite spiritless and unable to speak or stir, till by the care of his friend, and the application of the symbols of the holy mysteries, he was gradually restored to his strength and former health. From which time, as *Theodoret* adds, he had then persevered twenty-eight years in the same practice of fasting forty days in each year. During the first part of which days he used constantly to stand: and when through want of nourishment he grew too weak to endure that posture, he then began to sit; but at the last, was forced to lie down half dead and almost spent."

His next whim was, "to fix his perpetual station on the top of a pillar, whose circumference was hardly of two cubits; and after he had spent many years in that position, like a statue upon it's pedestal, on several different pillars, he mounted one at last thirty-six cubits high, and lived thirty years upon it; being placed in the middle region, as it were, between heaven and earth; where he conversed with God, and glorified him with angels; offering up for the men on earth his supplications to God, and drawing down from heaven the blessings of God upon men." But because these pillars allowed no other posture but that of standing, he contrived a method which enabled him to endure still the fatigue of his usual fasts. "For he got a beam fixed to the top of his pillar, to which he tied himself, and by that support held out the whole forty days without changing his position; till being strengthened by heaven with a larger measure of grace, he no longer wanted that help, but stood all the time, without tasting the least food, yet with ease and chearfulness."

The manner of passing his time on the pillar was this: "all the nights and days also, till three in the afternoon, were spent by him in prayer, in which he used continual bowings of his body, and always touched his very toes with his head. For this, says *Theodoret*, was easy to him, because he made but one meal in the week, and that a very light one, so that his belly being generally empty, gave him no obstruction in bending his back. One of those who stood by, looking upon him with *Theodoret*, had the curiosity to count the number of his bowings, but when he had counted to twelve hundred and forty-four, he was tired and would count them no longer. On solemn festivals, he stood with his hands stretched out towards heaven, from the setting of the sun to it's rising, without a wink of sleep the whole night.

"From three in the afternoon it was his practice to preach and to give divine lectures, to answer all quæstions and petitions which were offered to him, to cure diseases and to compose differences; but at sun-setting he began to converse again with God. He wrought innumerable miracles; giving health to the sick, children to the barren, and dispensing sacred oil to those likewise who desired it." To many of which miracles *Theodoret* declares himself to have been an eye-witness, as well as to his gift of prophecy, for he heard "him foretell a famine and a pestilence, and an irruption of locusts, and the death of one of *Theodoret's* enemies fifteen days before it happened." One of the miracles which *Theodoret* saw, was this: "an eminent *Ishmaelite* and believer in Christ, made a vow to God in the presence of *Symeon* that he would abstain from all animal food during the rest of his life; but being tempted afterwards to break his vow, he resolved to eat a fowl, and ordered it to be dressed for him accordingly; but when he sat down to eat, he found the flesh of it turned into stone. The barbarian, amazed at this miracle, ran away in all hast to the saint, proclaming his secret crime to all people, and imploring the saint, by the omnipotence of his prayers, to release him from the bond of this sin. There were many eye-witnesses of this miracle, who handled the fowl, and found the part of it about the breast to be compounded of bone and of stone."

By these miracles and austerities the fame of *Symeon*, as *Theodoret* says, was spread through the whole world; so that people of all nations and languages flocked to him in crouds from the remotest parts of the earth; from *Spain* and *Gaul*, and even *Britain* itself; and his name was so celebrated at *Rome*, *that the artificers of all kinds had little images of him placed in the entrance of their shops, as a guard and security to them against all sorts of mischief.*

This is the account in short of the Life of *Symeon Stylites*; the bare recital of which, tho' attested by ten *Theodorets*, must needs expose the absurdity of believing that it could in any manner be suggested or directed by divine inspiration. Yet Dr. *Chapman* contends, *that there is no better evidence for the very existence of* Symeon, *than we have for his miracles.* By which he means, I suppose, that we have the same evidence for both; the testimony of the same *Theodoret*, which he imagines to be as good in the one case as in the other: not reflecting that the same witness, of whatever character he be, will necessarily find a very different degree of credit, according to the different nature of the facts which he attests; and tho' credible in some, may be justly contemptible in others. For example, when we are told by *Theodoret*, and after him by *Evagrius*, that a certain monk called *Symeon*, who was personally known to them, took a fancy to live upon a pillar, where he was seen every day by many thousands; we have no reason to doubt of it; the thing was notorious; and there were many such enthusiasts in the same age; and every one of those thousands who saw him were as good witnesses of it as *Theodoret* himself. But when we are told by the same writers that *Symeon was inspired by God, and performed many things above the force of human nature*; this is a different case, which cannot command the same belief; being a matter of opinion, rather than of fact; of which very few could judge, fewer still be certain, and scarce one perhaps of all the thousands who saw him could be a competent witness: while the character of *Symeon* on the one side, and of *Theodoret* on the other, suggest many obvious reasons against the credibility of it.

To illustrate this more clearly by a similar instance from profane history. Two classical writers of undoubted credit, *Suetonius* and *Tacitus*, have each written the life and acts of the Emperor *Vespasian; who alone*, they say, *of all the Princes before him, was made a better man by his advancement to the Empire*. But the same writers also declare, that this good Emperor, *by a divine admonition from the God* Serapis, *publicly restored a blind man to his sight, and a cripple to his limbs, in the view of the people of* Alexandria; *and that many years after his death, when there was no reward or temptation for telling such a lie, several witnesses were still living who had seen those miracles performed, and bore testimony to the truth of them.* Now it is certain, that no body in any age ever doubted of the existence of *Vespasian*, yet many probably in all, and every single man in the present, not onely doubt but reject the story of his miracles; tho' these last be affirmed by the same writers who assure us of the first; to whose authority still we pay all the regard that is due, by believing them in every thing that is credible; in every thing of which they were competent witnesses; and charging the absurd and fabulous part to the superstition, prejudices, and false principles which prevailed in those ages.

The case is the same with *Theodoret* and all the Ecclesiastical Historians, who have transmitted to us the lives and miracles of the Monks, and other pious men of their own times. We take their word as far as reason and religion will permit us, and ascribe the rest to the credulity, the prejudices, and erroneous principles, which infected all the writers of those days. The Romanists indeed roundly embrace and espouse all the absurd and fictitious stories which they have delivered to us, and are under a necessity of doing so, since they teach the same corrupt doctrines, retain the same superstitious rites, and exercise the same usurped powers, for the sake of which those very stories were originally forged. But no Protestants, as far as I have observed, except the two Doctors above mentioned, have ever attempted to defend either the miracles or the principles of the fifth century; but on the contrary, have constantly signified either their suspicion or utter contempt of them.

Mr. *Dodwell*, whose piety and zeal for the honor of Christianity were as conspicuous as his learning, declares, "that nothing does so much discredit to the cause of miracles in general, among the Infidels and Atheists, as the impostures of the later ages; meaning the fourth, fifth, and following centuries. These, says he, they oppose to the undoubted credit of the earlier ages, and because these false prodigies deceived the whole world, they infer, that the ancient ones likewise, tho' false, might impose in the same manner upon the credulity of mankind."

Dr. *Cave*, the large extent of whose faith shines through every page of his writings, yet plainly intimates his suspicion of what *Theodoret* has attested concerning this very *Symeon*; for speaking of the amazing austerities which he practised, he adds, *moreover, if the Greek writers are to be regarded, he wrought innumerable miracles.*

Mr. *Collier* also, whose Ecclesiastical History shews, that miracles even of the grossest kind were of no hard digestion with him, could not yet digest these of our *Symeon*, but declares them to be wholly *fabulous, and such as render the truth itself suspected.*

Dr. *Hody*, so highly esteemed for his critical and theological learning, observes, "that stories concerning miracles are common to all the writers of lives, among the Christians of the middle ages, tho' otherwise good authors; and that the professed Historians themselves, as *Theodoret* and *Evagrius*, are full of relations, which were the result of a superstitious piety.

Since the most learned then as well as orthodox of our divines, and the most conversant also in Ecclesiastical antiquity, have so strongly signified their distrust both of the testimony of *Theodoret* and the particular acts of this *Symeon*, it is surprizing that Dr. *Chapman* should think it of service to Christianity, to lay so great a stress upon them, and in so peremptory a manner to vindicate the credit of miracles, whose sole tendency is to recommend, as a perfect pattern of the Christian life, the most extravagant enthusiasm and contemptible superstition that any age or history perhaps has ever produced. For that this was really the case, is evident from the writings of *Theodoret* himself, whose life of *Symeon Stylites* is a part onely of his *religious history*, as it is called, filled with the *lives of thirty Monks*, of the same class and character, distinguished by their peculiar austerities, and vying with each other who could invent the most whimsical methods and painful arts of mortifying their bodies.

One of these called *Baradatus*, contrived a sort of cage for his habitation, coarsely formed of lattice work, so wide and open as to expose him to all the inclemencies of the weather, and so low at the same time that it could not admit the full height of his body, but obliged him *to stand always in the posture of stooping*.

Another of them called *Thalaleus*, of a very bulky

size, suspended himself in the air, in a cage of a different kind, contrived by himself, and made so low and so strait also that it left him no more room than to sit with *his head perpetually bent down between his knees;* in which posture he had spent *ten years* when *Theodoret* first saw him. Yet all these ridiculous whims and extravagancies are considered by *Theodoret* as *the suggestions of the Holy Spirit,* and divine inventions, to baffle the artifices of the Devil; or so many *ladders,* as he tells us, *by which they mounted up to heaven;* and which were all confirmed by miracles as a proof of the divine approbation.

These were the wonder-workers, and these the miracles of the fifth century; the character of which Dr. *Chapman* summs up to this effect in the following articles.

1. That they were of a public nature, and performed in such a manner, as left no room for delusion.

2. That they were attended with beneficial effects, which could not possibly have gained credit, unless the strongest evidence of sense had proved them to be true.

3. That the end of them was not to confirm any idle errors or superstitions, but purely to advance the glory of truth and virtue.

4. That the accounts of them are given by men

of unquestionable integrity, piety, and learning, who were eye-witnesses of many of the facts, and declare in the most solemn manner that they knew them to be true.

5. That they were far from being vain and unnecessary, so as to render them doubtfull to after ages, but were attested by the strongest moral evidence, equal to that by which most of the ancient miracles are supported.

6. That they are incapable of giving any countenance to the fabulous pretences of the Papists; and that a Protestant of common capacity will discern as much difference between them and the Popish miracles, as between gold and brass, between light and darkness.

Yet from the short specimen of these miracles already given, and much more, from a full list of them, which, if it were required, may hereafter be given, the very contrary character of them, I am persuaded, will appear to be the true one, to all unprejudiced readers, in every one of those articles.

1. That they were all of such a nature, and performed in such a manner, as would necessarily inject a suspicion of fraud and delusion.

2. That the cures and beneficial effects of them, were either false, or imaginary, or accidental.

3. That they tend to confirm the idlest of all errors and superstitions.

4. That the integrity of the witnesses is either highly questionable, or their credulity at least so gross, as to render them unworthy of any credit.

5. That they were not onely vain and unnecessary, but generally speaking, so trifling also, as to excite nothing but contempt.

And lastly, that the belief and defence of them, are the onely means in the world that can possibly support, or that does in fact give any sort of countenance, to the modern impostures in the Romish Church.

Then as to the Monks also, who are said to have wrought those miracles, the Doctor is not less zealous in defending and extolling all their extravagancies. He declares, "that they were intended for the best and most excellent purposes. That all the friends to Christianity must think, that in their voluntary austerities, they shewed such prudence, virtue, and greatness of mind, as deserve the highest encomiums of posterity. And that the ancient Monasteries were very different from the modern, quite remote from the corruptions of Popery, and deserving the approbation of the strictest Protestants." Yet for my own part, notwithstanding all his panegyric on those primitive Monks and monasteries, I shall not scruple to own, 1st, That I look upon the whole institution of monkery, from what age or what Saint soever it drew it's origin, to be contrary not onely to the principles of the Gospel, but to the interests of all civil society, and the chief source of all the corruptions which have ever since infested the Christian Church. 2dly, That by all which I have ever read of the old, and have seen of the modern Monks, I take the preference to be clearly due to the last, as having a more regular discipline, more good learning, and less superstition among them than the first.

Before we take leave of this subject, I shall just add a word or two concerning the character of *Theodoret* himself, to whose testimony Dr. *Chapman* pays so extraordinary a regard, and whose authority he declares to be decisive in the case before us. The learned Mons. *Du Pin*, in his account of him, extracted from his writings, says, "that he was born at *Antioch*, A.D. 386; that his birth was accompanied by miracles, both before and after it, which he himself relates in his religious history: that, *if we may believe him*, his mother was healed of an incurable disease in her eye by one *Peter* a Monk; that upon the prayers of another Monk, called *Macedonius*, God granted her to conceive a son, after thirteen years of barrenness, and to bring him safely into the world: that by the prayers of the first of those Monks, *Peter*, she was preserved also from death after her delivery; and that her husband and her son had often felt the effects of *Peter's* virtue and sanctity, and were cured of their distempers by touching onely his girdle."

This account, I say, is drawn from *Theodoret* himself; whence we learn, that he was nursed and trained in all the bigottry and superstition with which that age abounded; taught from his very cradle to venerate Monks and their miracles; and made to believe, with the first knowledge which he received, that he owed his very existence to the efficacy of their prayers. He tells us, "that his mother sent him once every week to beg the blessing of the Monk, *Peter*; and that he went as often also to receive the instructions and benediction of the other Monk, *Macedonius*, who never failed to remind him of the great pains which it had cost to bring him into the world, and how many nights he had spent in praying to God for nothing else but his birth." And as *Theodoret* is said to have been very tenacious of the principles which he had once imbibed, so it was his constant practice through his whole life to visit the cells and habitations of all the celebrated Monks of those times, with whose lives and miracles he has filled his *religious history*; from which I shall here transcribe a story or two, out of the great number which he has recorded, of the same sort and of his own knowledge, as a specimen both of the judgement and the fidelity of the compiler.

In his life of the Monk, *Peter*, he declares, "that his very garments wrought wonders like to those of St. *Paul*; which I do not mention, says he, by way of hyperbole, but with the testimony of truth for what I am saying. For his girdle, made of coarse linnen, being very broad and long, he cut it into two parts, with the one of which he girded his own loins, and mine with the other. This last my mother has often applied to me and to my father, when we were sick, and driven away our distempers by it, and made use of it also herself, as a remedy for her own health. Many of our acquaintance, who knew this, frequently borrowed the girdle for the service of other sick people, and always found the same good effects of it's virtue; till a certain person, who borrowed it, ungratefull to his benefactors, never restored it, and so we were deprived of the benefit of this gift."

In the life of another Monk, called *James*, he tells this story, "that the reliques of some of the ancient *Patriarchs*, *Prophets*, and *Apostles*, were brought to him in a chest from *Phœnicia* and *Palæstine*, and received by a public procession of all the orders of the Clergy and the Layety. But the Monk *James* did not think fit to assist at this solemnity, having conceived some doubts, it seems, whether the reliques, said to be *John Baptist's*, were really so or not. Upon which, in the night following, as he was praying, there appeared to him a certain person cloathed in white, and demanded of him, *why he did not come out to meet them?* and when *James* asked who they were of whom he spake; he replied, those who came the other day from *Phœnicia* and *Palæstine*. The next night also the same person appeared to him again; and in order to remove all his scruples, brought along with him St. *John Baptist* and the *Patriarch Joseph*, who were severally presented to him, and held discourse with him on the subject of their reliques." With these stories, I shall leave it to the reader to determine, whether a writer of this turn and character can reasonably be thought unprejudiced, and of an authority uncontestable, or worthy indeed of any credit at all, where the honor of Monks, and the reality of their miracles are the points in question.

The same Mons. *Du Pin*, after he has given us an abstract of Theodoret's *religious History*, adds the following reflection: "this History contains many things remarkable concerning the discipline of this time. By it we see that great honor was given to the Saints; that they were invoked; that men expected to be helped by their prayers; that their reliques were sought after with great earnestness; that people believed very easily in them; attributed great virtue and many miracles to them; and were very credulous, &c." But tho' the whole turn and purpose of *Theodoret's sacred History* tends to strengthen the interest of the Romish, and to hurt the credit of the Protestant cause, by celebrating the forged miracles of *Monks, and Saints, and reliques, and holy water, and sacred oil,* it is curious to observe with what a different temper the popish writer, Mons. *Du Pin*, and the protestant writer, Dr. *Chapman*, have each expressed themselves on the subject of his testimony. The papist, candidly imitating his doubts, says, *if we may believe* Theodoret, such and such miracles were performed. The protestant on the contrary, contemning all doubts, declares, *that we must believe him, that his evidence is uncontestable, that to reject it is to destroy the faith of history.*

The fortunes of these two writers were as different also as their principles: the candor of the Papist being thought too favourable to Protestantism, was censured and disgraced by the Popish Bishops; the zeal of the Protestant, tending directly to Popery, was extolled and rewarded by the Protestant Bishops.

We have dwelt already so long on the miracles of the fifth century, that it must be needless to examine the particular merit of that miracle which Dr. *Berriman* has so accurately defended. I shall employ therefore but a very few words upon it. The story is this: "*Hunneric the Vandal,* a Christian Prince of the *Arian heresy,* in his persecution of the orthodox party in *Africa,* ordered the tongues of a certain society of them to be cut out to the roots; but by a surprizing instance of God's good Providence, they were enabled to speak articulately and distinctly without their tongues; and so continuing to make open profession of the same doctrine, they became not onely the preachers, but living witnesses of it's truth, and a perpetual rebuke to the *Arian* faction." This miracle is attested by several contemporary writers, who affirm that they had seen and heard some of those Confessors *speaking distinctly, after they had lost their tongues.*

Now it may not improbably be supposed on this occasion, that tho' their tongues were ordered to be cut out to the roots, and are said to have been so cut, yet the sentence might not be so strictly executed, as not to leave in some of them such a share of that organ, as was sufficient, in a tolerable degree, for the use of speech. It is remarkable also, that two of this company are said to have utterly lost the faculty of speaking, who had been deprived perhaps of their entire tongues: for tho' this be ascribed to the peculiar judgement of God, for a punishment of the immoralities, of which they were afterwards guilty, yet that seems to be a forced and improbable solution of the matter. We are told likewise, that another of these Confessors *who had been dumb from his birth, yet by losing his tongue with the rest, acquired also the use of speech:* which is a circumstance so singular and extraordinary, that it carries with it a suspicion of art and contrivance, to enhance the luster of the miracle.

But to come still more close to the point. If we should allow after all, that the tongues of these confessors were cut away to the very roots; what will the learned doctor say, if this boasted miracle, which he so strenuously defends, should be found at last to be no miracle at all? The tongue indeed has generally been considered as absolutely necessary to the use of speech: so that to hear men talk without it, might easily pass for a miracle in that credulous age; especially when it gave so illustrious a confirmation to the orthodox faith, and so signal an overthrow to the *Arian heresy*. Yet the opportunities of examining the truth of the case by experiment have been so rare in the world, that there was always room to doubt whether there was any thing miraculous in it or not. But we have an instance in the present century, indisputably attested, and published about thirty years ago, which clears up all our doubts, and intirely decides the question. I mean the case of a *girl born without a tongue, who yet talked as distinctly and easily as if she had enjoyed the full benefit of that organ*: a particular account of which is given in the *Memoires of the Academy of Sciences* at Paris, drawn up by an eminent physician who had carefully examined the mouth of the girl and all the several parts of it, in order to discover by what means her speech was performed without the help of a tongue; which he has there explained with great skill and accuracy. In the same account he refers us likewise to another instance, published about eighty years before, by a *surgeon of Saumur*, of a boy, *who at the age of eight or nine years, lost his tongue by a gangrene or ulcer, occasioned by the small pox, yet retained the faculty of speaking*, in the same manner as the girl.

Let our Doctor then defend this miracle with all the power of his zeal and learning: let him urge the testimonies of *senators, chancellors, bishops, archbishops, and popes*; of persons, *who had too much learning and judgement*, he says, *to be deceived in so important a fact, tho' they lived an hundred years after it*; of *Æneas* also of *Gaza*, *who opened their very mouths*, as he tells us, *to make his observations with more exactness*. Yet the humble testimony of this single physician, grounded on real experiment, will overturn at once all his pompous list of dignified authorities, and convince every man of judgement that this pretended miracle, like all the other fictions which have been imposed upon the world under that character, owed it's whole credit to our ignorance of the powers of nature.

In short, when we reflect on the corrupt and degennerate state of the Church in the end of the fourth century, allowed by the most diligent inquirers into antiquity, and that this age was the pattern to all that succeded it, in which the same corruptions were not onely practised, but agreeably to the nature of all corruption, carried still to a greater excess, and improved from bad to worse down to the time of the reformation; we may safely conclude, without weighing the particular scruples which may arise upon each single miracle, that they were all, in the gross, of the same class and species,—the mere effects of fraud and imposture. For we can hardly dip into any part of ecclesiastical history, of what age soever, without being shocked by the attestation of several, which from the mere incredibility of them appear at first sight to be fabulous. This is confessed on all sides, even by the warmest defenders of the primitive Fathers, and cannot be accounted for in any other way than by ascribing it to the experience which those Fathers, had of the blind credulity and superstition of the ages in which they lived, and which had been trained by them to consider *the impossibility of a thing as an argument for the belief of it.* But in whatever light we contemplate these stories, whether as believed, or as forged by them, or as affirmed onely and not believed, it necessarily destroys their credit in all other miraculous relations whatsoever. Yet it is surprizing to see with what ease the advocates of these miracles overlook and contemn all reflections of this kind, and think it sufficient to tell us, that *the Fathers, tho' honest, were apt to be very credulous:* for with these disputants, credulity it seems, how gross soever, casts not the least slur upon their testimony; which in all cases, where it does not confute itself by it's own extravagance, they maintain to be convincing and decisive, and superior to all suspicion. Whereas the sole inference which reason would teach us to draw from an attestation of miracles so conspicuously fabulous, is, that the same witnesses are not to be trusted in any; as being either incapable from a weakness of judgement of discerning the truth and probability of things, or determined by craft and fraud to defend every thing that was usefull to them. In a word; in all inquiries of this nature we may take it for a certain rule, that those who are conscious of the power of working true miracles, can never be tempted either to invent, or to propagate, any which are false; because the detection of any one would taint the credit of all the rest, and defeat the end proposed by them. But impostors are naturally drawn, by a long course of success, into a security which puts them off their guard, and tempts them gradually, out of mere wantonness and contempt of those whom they had so frequently deluded, to stretch their frauds beyond the bounds of probability, till by repeated acts of this kind they tire the patience of the most credulous, and expose their tricks to the scorn even of the populace.

I have now thrown together all which I had collected for the support of my argument, or as much at least as I thought sufficient to illustrate the real state of the primitive miracles: and if we cast up the summ of all that boasted evidence, which the *unanimity of the Fathers, the tradition of the Catholic Church, and the faith of history,* have produced at last on the other side, towards the confirmation of the said miracles, we shall find the whole to amount in reality to no proof at all. For to run over them all again in short:

The gift of *raising the dead* is affirmed onely by the single authority of *Irenæus,* Bishop of *Lyons;* and was either not known, or not believed at least, in the very same age, by another Bishop, full as venerable, *Theophilus* of *Antioch.* The *gift of tongues,* which rests likewise on the single testimony of the same *Irenæus,* is confuted even by himself, who complains of his own want of it in the very work of propagating the Gospel. The *gift of expounding the Scriptures,* which is reckoned commonly with the rest, and clamed in particular by *Justin Martyr,* is allowed to have had no subsistence at all in any age, or any writer of the primitive Church. The *gift of casting out Devils,* the most celebrated of them all, is reduced to nothing, by the accounts even of the ancients themselves, which plainly testify that it had no effect in many cases, and could not work a perfect cure in any. And as to other diseases, where oil especially was applied, they might probably enough be cured without a miracle; or by the same arts with which the same cures were performed among the heathens: which, tho' the undoubted effects of fraud, were yet managed so dexterously, as to be constantly ascribed by the Christians to the power of Dæmons. Lastly, *the gift of prophetic visions and trances,* was of a kind which could not easily be proved to the satisfaction of any; was of no service therefore to the propagation of the Gospel, or the conviction of unbelievers; being wholly exercised among the Christians themselves, and owing it's chief credit to heretics and enthusiasts; and always suspected by the sober and judicious: so that after florishing for a while through a visionary generation or two, it presently after fell into utter contempt.

This then being the real state of the miracles of the primitive Church, I freely commit them once more to the *Chapmans*, the *Berrimans*, and the *Stebbings*, to defend and enjoy them as much as they please; happy without doubt, in this sceptical age, to find themselves blessed with that heroic faith which can remove mountains, and beat down every obstacle which sense, or reason, or fact can possibly oppose to it. Dr. *Chapman* has declared beforehand, *that whenever my larger work should appear, the primitive Fathers would find greater friends to their memory, and abler advocates to their cause, than I would wish to exist.* That time is now come, and those abler advocates expected; but let them appear when they will, I am so far from grudging their help to the Fathers, that I wish them the ablest which Popery itself can afford: for Protestantism, I am sure, can supply none whom they would chuse to retain in their cause; none who can defend them, without contradicting their own profession, and disgracing their own character; or produce anything but what deserves to be laughed at, rather than answered. I must however except one, who acts indeed with a better grace and more consistency: for when I had treated him by mistake as a *Protestant*, he flatly disowns the name, and calls himself a *Catholic Christian*; the same title which a Popish writer had before assumed, in his remarks on my *Letter from Rome*; and what all these advocates, who hang as it were between the two religions, affect to assume, that they may evade for a while the more invidious name of Papist.

V. All that remains towards the final confirmation of my argument, is, to refute, as I promised, some of the most plausible objections which have been made to it by my antagonists; and which by humouring the prejudices and prepossessions of many pious Christians, seem the most likely to make an impression to it's disadvantage.

Sect. 1. In the first place then it is objected, that by the character which I have given of the ancient Fathers, *the authority of the books of the New Testament*, which were transmitted to us through their hands, will be rendered *precarious and uncertain*.

To which I answer, that the objection is trifling and groundless, and that the authority of those books does not depend upon the faith of the Fathers, or of any particular set of men, but on the general credit and reception which they found, not onely in all the Churches, but with all the private Christians of those ages who were able to purchase copies of them; among whom, tho' it might perhaps be the desire of a few to corrupt, yet it was the common interest of all to preserve, and of none to destroy them.

And we find accordingly, that they were guarded by all with the strictest care, so as to be conceled from the knowledge and search of their heathen adversaries, who alone were desirous to extirpate them. After such a publication therefore, and wide dispersion of them from their very origin, it is hardly possible that they should either be corrupted, or suppressed, or counterfeited by a few, of what character or abilities soever; or that, according to the natural course of things, they should not be handed down from age to age, in the same manner, with the works of all the other ancient writers of *Greece* and *Rome*, which, tho' transmitted through the hands of many profligate and faithless generations of men, yet have suffered no diminution of their credit on that account: for tho' in every age there were several perhaps, who from crafty and selfish motives, might be disposed to deprave, or even to suppress some particular books, yet their malice could reach onely to a few copies, and would be restrained therefore from the attempt, or corrected at least after the attempt, by the greater number of the same books, which were out of their reach and remained still incorrupt. But besides all this, there were some circumstances peculiar to the books of the New Testament, which insured the preservation of them more effectually than of any other ancient books whatsoever; the divinity of their character; and the religious regard which was paid to them by all the sects and parties of Christians; and above all, the mutual jealousies of those very parties, which were perpetually watching over each other, lest any of them should corrupt the sources of that pure doctrine which they all professed to teach and to deduce from the same books. Let the craft therefore of the ancient Fathers be as great as we can suppose it to be; let it be capable of adding some of their own forgeries for a while to the canon of Scripture; yet it was not in the power of any craft to impose spurious pieces in the room of those genuin ones, which were actually deposited in all Churches, and preserved with the utmost reverence in the hands of so many private Christians.

But I may go a step farther, and venture to declare, that if we should allow the objection to be true, it cannot in any manner hurt my argument; for if it be natural and necessary that the craft and credulity of witnesses should always detract from the credit of their testimony, who can help it? or on what is the consequence to be charged, but on that nature and constitution of things from which it flows? or if the authority of any books be really weakened by the character which I have given of the Fathers, will it follow from thence that the character must necessarily be false, and that the Fathers were neither crafty nor credulous? That surely can never be pretended; because the craft and credulity which are charged upon them must be determined by another sort of evidence; not by consequences, but by facts; and if the charge be confirmed by these, it must be admitted as true, how far soever the consequences may reach.

Sect. 2. It has been alledged "that all suspicion of fraud in the case of the primitive miracles seems to be precluded by that public appeal and challenge which the Christian Apologists make to their enemies the Heathens, to come and see with their own eyes the reality of the facts which they attest." But this objection, tho' it may seem plausible indeed to a common reader, yet to all who are acquainted with the condition of the Christians in those days, and the difficulty of making their apologies known to the world, will be found to have no real weight in it. The Gospel indeed soon began to make a considerable progress among the vulgar, and to gain some few also of a more distinguished rank, yet continued to be held in such contempt by the generality of the better sort, through the three first centuries, that they scarce ever thought it worth while to make any inquiry about it, or to examine the merit of it's pretensions. The principal writers of *Rome*, who make any mention of the Christians, about the time of *Trajan*, plainly shew, that they knew nothing more of them, or their religion, than what they had picked up, as it were, by chance, from the gross misrepresentation of common fame, and speak of them accordingly, as *a set of despicable, stubborn, and even wicked Enthusiasts.*

Suetonius calls them *a race of men of a new and mischievous superstition.* And *Tacitus*, describing the horrible tortures which they suffered under *Nero*, for the pretended crime of burning the City of *Rome*, says, "that they were detested for their flagitious practices; possessed with an abominable superstition; and condemned, not so much for their supposed crime of setting fire to the City, as for the hatred of all mankind; and tho' they deserved the most exemplary punishments, yet it raised some pity towards them, to see them so miserably destroyed, not on the account of the public utility, but to satiate the cruelty of a single man."

Pliny also, when he was the Governor of a Province, in which the Christians were very numerous, and under an actual persecution in the reign of *Trajan*, yet in his celebrated letter to that Emperor concerning them, declares, "that he had never been present at any of their examinations, and did not so much as know for what they were punished, or how far they deserved punishment: that by all the enquiries which he had since made, he could not discover any practices among them, but what were harmless and innocent.—And nothing, in short, but a wretched and extravagant superstition, which had spread itself very wide, among persons of both sexes, of every age and condition, which might however be subdued by gentler methods; by moderating the rigor of the persecution, and pardoning the penitent; by which lenity, great numbers of them had already been recalled to their ancient worship."

This is the whole account which we have of the Primitive Christians, from the best Heathen writers, to the time of *Antoninus Pius*: in whose reign, and that of his Successor, *M. Aurelius*, the ancient Apologies of *Justin Martyr*, *Melito*, and *Athenagoras*, were addressed to the Emperor and Senate of *Rome*: notwithstanding which, their condition, generally speaking, continued much the same through the following ages, till they were established at last by the civil power: during all which time they were constantly insulted and calumniated by their Heathen Adversaries, as a *stupid, credulous, impious sect; the scum of mankind, and the prey of crafty Impostors:* calumnies, of which all the ancient Apologists complain, and take great pains to confute. *Tertullian* expostulates very warmly with the Heathen Magistrates, "that they would not give themselves the trouble to make the least inquiry into their manners and doctrines; but condemned them for the mere name, without examination or trial; treating a Christian of course, as guilty of every crime; *as an enemy of the Gods, Emperors, laws, customs, and even of nature itself*—and what, says he, can be more unjust than to hate what you know nothing of, even tho' it deserved to be hated?" *Arnobius* and *Lactantius* make the same complaint near an hundred years later, in the beginning of the fourth century, that they were derided every where by the Gentiles, *as a senseless, stupid race of blockheads and brutes, to whose impieties, all the calamities, which afflicted the several countries where they lived, were constantly imputed.*

In these circumstances, it cannot be imagined, that men of figure and fortunes would pay any attention to the apologies or writings of a sect so utterly despised; especially, when on the one hand, there was no elegance of stile or composition to invite them to read; and on the other, all the discouragements, which the Government could give, to deter them from reading. Much less can we believe that the Emperor and Senate of *Rome* should take any notice of those Apologies, or even know indeed that any such were addressed to them. For should the like case happen in our days, that any Methodist, Moravian, or French Prophet, should publish an apology for his brethren, addressed to the King and the Parliament, is it not wholly improbable, that the Government would pay any regard to it, or take it at all into their consideration? How can it then be supposed, that the Emperor and Senate of *Rome*, who had a worse opinion of the ancient Christians than we of our modern Fanatics, and instead of tolerating were using all methods to destroy them, would give themselves the trouble to read, or to consider the merit of their writings?

We must add to all this, the great difficulty of publishing books, or of making them known to the world in those ages. The ease, which we now find in providing and dispersing what number of copies we please, by the opportunity of the press, make us apt to imagine, without considering the matter, that the publication of books was the same easy affair in all former times as in the present But the case was quite different. For when there were no books in the world but what were written out by hand, with great labor and expence, the method of publishing them was necessarily very slow and the price very dear, so that the rich onely and curious would be disposed or able to purchase them; and to such also, it was often difficult to procure them, or to know even where they were to be bought.

In the Epistle of the Church of *Smyrna*, mentioned above, concerning the Martyrdom of *St. Poly-*

carp, there is a passage or two which will help to confirm what I am now asserting. For towards the end of it, the *Philadelphians*, to whom it is addressed, are desired, as soon as they have informed themselves of the contents, *to send it forward to all the other brethren*, who lived more remote, or beyond *Philadelphia*, that they also might read it and glorify God. The note likewise, which is annexed to the end of the Epistle, declares, "that the copy of this most valued piece, which had been transcribed from the book of *Irenæus*, had lain buried and unknown at *Corinth* for several ages, almost destroyed by time, and in danger of being lost to the world, till it was discovered by a revelation from *Polycarp* himself, made to one *Pionius*," from whose transcript all the copies of it now extant are derived. These passages, I say, plainly intimate, how difficult it must have been to the Christians of those days, to provide such books as were wanted even for their own use, and much more to disperse such a number of them as was sufficient for the information of the public.

Since this then was the condition of publishing books in those primitive ages, in which the Christians were neither able to bear the expence of copying, nor the Heathens disposed to buy them, there is great reason to believe, that their Apologies, how gravely soever addressed to Emperors and Senates, lay concealed and unknown to the public for many years, in a few private hands, and among the faithful onely; especially, when the publication of them was not onely difficult and expensive, but so criminal also, as to expose them often to danger, and even to capital punishment; and when the books themselves, as oft as they were found by the magistrate, instead of being read, were generally ordered to be burnt.

Sect. 3. It is urged against me, "that no suspicion of craft can reasonably be entertained against persons of so exalted a piety, who exposed themselves to persecution and even to Martyrdom, in confirmation of the truth of what they taught." But this likewise will appear to have as little solidity in it as the former. For all who are conversant with history know, that nothing gives so invincible a prejudice, and so strong a biass to the mind of man, as religious zeal in favor of every thing that is thought useful to the object which excites it. And the several facts, which I have already stated, will inable us to judge, in what manner the extraordinary zeal of those ancients may be presumed to have operated in the case now in question. I shall say nothing more therefore on that head; but since some of those Fathers, to whose testimony I have chiefly appealed, as *Papias*, *Justin*, *Irenæus*, *Cyprian*, &c., were not onely persons of the greatest piety and zeal, but said to have been Martyrs also for the faith of Christ, it may be proper to add a reflection or two on the particular case of Martyrdom, in order to shew that this venerable name made no real difference in the personal characters of men, nor ought to give any additional weight to the authority of a Christian witness.

There were various motives of different kinds, as

Mr. *Dodwell* has shewn, which would naturally induce the primitive Christians not onely to indure but even to wish and aspire to Martyrdom. He observes, "that among the ancient *Jews*, the *Galilæans* were remarkable for the obstinacy of their temper and a contempt of death; whose example, he imagines, might have some influence on those first Christians, who drew their origin from that country, and were constantly called *Galilæans*, and charged with the same spirit of obstinacy by their adversaries." A character which seems to be particularly verified in the Christians of *Palæstine*, concerning whom, *Tiberianus*, the Governor of *Syria*, sends the following account to the Emperor *Trajan*.

"I am quite tired with punishing and destroying the *Galilæans*, or those of the sect called Christians, according to your orders. Yet they never cease to profess voluntarily what they are, and to offer themselves to death. Wherefore I have labored by exhortations and threats to discourage them from daring to confess to me that they are of that Sect. Yet in spite of all persecution they continue still to do it. Be pleased therefore to let me know what your highness thinks proper to be done with them."

Glory also, or reputation, was another great spur to Martyrdom; for by the principles of those ages, nothing was esteemed more glorious than the *crown of Martyrdom*, as it was called. There was an anniversary festival instituted to the honor of each Martyr; in which their memories were celebrated by panegyrical orations, and a veneration, next to divine, paid to their reliques. In their prisons they were visited by the Christians of all ranks, proud to minister to them in the very lowest offices, and to kiss their chains; and if they happened to escape with life from their tortures, as they frequently did, their authority was ever after most highly respected in the decision of all controversies; in absolving men from the ordinary discipline of the Church, in granting pardon to lapsed Christians, and restoring them to communion, on what terms they thought fit.

But the principal incentive to Martyrdom, was the assurance not onely of an immortality of glory and happiness in another world, in common with all other pious Christians, but of extraordinary and distinguished rewards, and a degree of happiness proportionable to the degree of their sufferings. For while the souls of ordinary Christians were to wait their doom in some intermediate state, or pass to their final bliss through a purgation by fire, it was a general belief, that the Martyrs were admitted *to the immediate fruition of Paradise, and that the fire of Martyrdom purged all their sins away at once.* And the opinion likewise which commonly prevailed in these days, that this world was near to it's end, made them the more eager still to snatch that crown which would intitle them to such high privileges; give them a power with God, so as to procure benefits for others, and make them Assessors and Judges with Christ himself at the last day.

There was another notion, diligently inculcated and generally believed at the same time, which was sufficient of itself to efface all the terrors of Martyrdom, *viz.*, that under all that dreadfull apparatus of racks and fires, and the seeming atrocity of their tortures, the Martyrs were miraculously freed from all sense of pain, nay, felt nothing but transports of joy from the cruelty of their tormentors. All which is expressly affirmed by many of the ecclesiastical writers. *The visible assistance of heaven,* says Dr. *Chapman, relieving the pains of some, extinguishing them in others, and converting them into pleasure and rapture in many—which facts,* he declares, *to be so well known and so well attested; so plain and so indisputable, that there was no occasion for him to take the trouble of proving them.* *Socrates*, the Historian, has furnished an instance of them in the case of one *Theodorus;* and the old Martyrologies, as they are published by the Romanists, and especially *the Acts of Perpetua and Felicitas,* to which the Doctor refers us for the indisputable proof of true miracles, will supply us with many more. This *Theodorus* was a young Christian, of eminent zeal and piety, who is said to have suffered the most cruel tortures by the command of the Emperor *Julian;* but after he was left for dead by his tormentors, was providentially preserved and restored to life. "*Ruffinus* happening to meet with him many years after, took occasion to ask him whether he had been sensible of any very sharp pains under the agony of his torture; to which he answered, that he had felt but very little, and that a certain young person stood by him all the time, wiping away the sweat which flowed from him, strengthening his mind, and filling him with delight rather than torment, during his continuance on the rack."

Lastly, we must add to these several motives, the scandal of flying from persecution, and the infamy which attended the lapsed Christians, so as to make life hardly supportable to those, who through fear of the rack and a cruel death, had been tempted to deny their faith, or guilty of any compliance with the idolatry of their persecutors. All which topics, when displayed with art and eloquence by their ablest teachers, were sufficient to inflame the multitude to what pitch of zeal they pleased, so as to make them even provoke and offer themselves forwardly to the most dreadful torments. "Who is there," says *Cyprian*, "who would not strive with all his might to arrive at so great a glory, to be a friend of God, enter into present joy with Christ, and after earthly torments receive heavenly rewards? If it be glorious to worldly soldiers, after conquering an enemy, to return triumphant into their country, how much greater glory is it, after having vanquished the Devil, to return triumphant into paradise, whence *Adam* was expelled, and there to erect trophies over that very enemy who expelled him? To accompany God, when he comes to take vengeance on his enemies; to be placed at his side when he sits in judgment; to be made coheirs with Christ; equal with Angels; and together with *the Apostles, Prophets, and Patriarchs*, to rejoice in the possession of an Heavenly Kingdom. These things you are to bear in your minds and memories. What persecution can get the better of such meditations? what torments be superior to them?"

These principles and motives, I say, had such

force as sometimes to animate even bad men to indure a Martyrdom. For the Heretics also had their Martyrs, as all history informs us, as well as the Orthodox; who yet in their common sufferings and death, continued to testify their mutual aversion, *and to refuse all communion with each other*. But by bad men, who became Martyrs, I do not mean such onely as were called Heretics, for that name was often given even to the best; but the proud, the contentious, the drunken, and the lewd, among the orthodox Martyrs themselves: of all which kinds there were many, as *St. Cyprian* complains, who, after they had nobly sustained the trial of Martyrdom, and escaped with life from the torments of their persecutors, yet by a petulant, factious, and profligate behaviour, gave great scandal and disturbance to the discipline of the Church.

This is expressly declared by *Cyprian* in several of his letters: in one of which, addressed to the whole body of the Confessors, after he has signified his joy, "that the greatest part of them were made the better by the honor of their confession, and preserved their glory, by a quiet and inoffensive carriage, yet he had been informed, he says, of others, who infected their society, and disgraced the laudable name of Confessor by their evil conversation: some of them being drunken and lascivious, some puffed up and swollen with pride; while others, as he had heard with the utmost grief, defiled their bodies, the temples of God, sanctified by their confession, with the promiscuous and infamous use of lewd women." In one of his letters also to the Clergy, he says, I am grieved when I hear how some of them run about, wickedly and insolently spending their time in trifles, or in sowing discord, and defiling the members of Christ, and which have already confessed Christ, by the unlawfull use of women." And in another treatise, where he is touching the same subject, "let no man wonder, says he, that some of the Confessors commit such horrible and grievous sins; for confession does not secure them from the snares and temptations of the Devil—otherwise we should never after see any frauds, and whoredoms and adulteries in Confessors, which I now groan and grieve to see in some of them."

It is not my design, by what is said here on the subject of Martyrdom, to detract in any manner from the real merit and just praise of those primitive Martyrs, who with an invincible constancy, sustained the cause of Christ, at the expense of their lives. It is reasonable to believe, that, generally speaking, they were the best sort of Christians, distinguished by their exemplary zeal and piety, and the chief ornaments of the Church in their several ages; yet it is certain that they were subject still to the same passions, prejudices, and errors, which were common to all the other pious Christians of the same age. My sole view therefore is to expose the vanity of those extravagant honors, and that idolatrous worship, which are paid to them indiscriminately by the Church of *Rome;* and to shew especially, that the circumstance of their Martyrdom, while it gives the strongest proof of the sincerity of their faith and trust in the promises of the Gospel, adds nothing to the character of their knowledge or their sagacity; nor, consequently, any weight to their testimony, in preference to that of any other just and devout Christian whatsoever.

Sect. 4. It has been frequently objected by my Antagonists, that to reject the unanimous testimony of the Fathers, in their reports of the primitive miracles, will destroy the faith and credit of all history.

This was the constant cant of all the zealots, even of the Heathen world, whenever any of their established superstitions were attacked by men of sense. "If these things, they cried, approved by the wisdom of our ancestors, and confirmed by the consent of ages, can be shewn at last to be false, we must burn all our annals, and believe nothing at all." And the same outcry, as *Eusebius* tells us, was made by them also against the Christians, when the Gospel first began to spread itself among them: "that to reject a belief and worship universally established by Kings, Legislators, and Philosophers of all nations, whether *Greeks* or *Barbarians*, was an impious apostacy from the rites of their ancestors, and a contradiction to the sense and judgement of mankind." The Christians on the other hand constantly derided this plea, and declared, "that to follow the inventions of their ancestors without any judgement or examination, and to be led perpetually by others, like brute animals, was to preclude themselves from that search of wisdom and knowledge, which is natural to man." Yet when it came at last to their own turn, to find the authority of ages on their side, they took up the same plea which they had before rejected; and urge it at this day as the principal objection to Protestantism; that it is a *mere novelty*, which had no existence in the world before *Luther*, contradictory to the practice of all the primitive Saints and Martyrs of the Catholic Church, and to the unanimous consent of fifteen centuries."

If this objection therefore had ever been found to have any force in it, the ancient Christians could never have over-ruled the impostures of Paganism; nor our Reformers, the superstitions of Popery. But in truth, when it comes to be seriously considered, it will appear to have no sense at all in it; and if the Doctors *Chapman* and *Berriman*, who now revive and so zealously urge it, were called upon to explane themselves upon it, they would find it difficult, I dare say, to tell us what they mean by it. If they mean that a contempt of those miracles which they would persuade us to believe, would necessarily derive the same contempt on history itself, all experience has shewn the contrary; for tho' there have been doubters and contemners of such miracles in all ages, yet history has maintained it's ground through them all. During the three first centuries, the whole world in a manner not onely doubted, but rejected the miracles of the primitive Christians; yet history was written and read with the same pleasure and profit as before, and applied by the unbelievers themselves to the confirmation of their very doubts. Our commerce with the times past, as they are represented to us in history, is of much the same kind with our manner of dealing with the present. We find many men in the world, whose fidelity we have just ground to suspect; yet a number of others, whom we can readily trust, sufficient to support that credit and mutual confidence by which the business of life is carried on. Just so in ancient history; we find many things of which we have cause to doubt, many which we are obliged to reject; yet it's use still subsists, and from real and indisputable facts supplies sufficient matter both of instruction and entertainment to every judicious reader.

If our Doctors therefore mean any thing by the objection which we are examining, it must be this; that the same principle which induces us to suspect the primitive miracles, and particularly those of *Symeon Stylites,* when so forcibly and credibly attested, must induce us also, if we are consistent with ourselves, to suspect every thing that is delivered to us from ancient history. But they widely mistake the matter, and do not at all reflect on what I have intimated above, that the history of miracles is of a kind totally different from that of common events; the one, to be suspected always of course, without the strongest evidence to confirm it; the other, to be admitted of course, without as strong reason to suspect it. Ordinary facts, related by a credible person, furnish no cause of doubting from the nature of the thing; but if they be strange and extraordinary, doubts naturally arise, and in proportion as they approach towards the marvellous, those doubts still increase and grow stronger. For mere honesty will not warrant them; we require other qualities in the historian; a degree of knowledge, experience, and discernment, sufficient to judge of the whole nature and circumstances of the case: and if any of these be wanting, we necessarily suspend our belief. A weak man indeed, if honest, may attest common events as credibly as the wisest; yet can hardly make any report that is credible of such as are miraculous; because a suspicion will always occur that his weakness, and imperfect knowledge of the extent of human art, had been imposed upon by the craft of cunning jugglers. On the other hand, should a man of known abilities and judgement relate to us things miraculous, or undertake to perform them himself, the very notion of his skill, without an assurance also of his integrity, would excite onely the greater suspicion of him; especially if he had any interest to promote, or any favorite opinion to recommend, by the authority of such works: because a pretension to miracles has, in all ages and nations, been found the most effectual instrument of impostors, towards deluding the multitude, and gaining their ends upon them.

There is not a single historian of antiquity, whether Greek or Latin, who has not recorded *oracles, prodigies, prophecies, and miracles,* on the occasion of some memorable events, or revolutions of states and kingdoms. Many of these are attested in the gravest manner and by the gravest writers, and were firmly believed at the time by the populace: yet it is certain, that there is not one of them which we can reasonably take to be genuin: not one, but what was either wholly forged, or from the opportunity of some unusual circumstance attending it, improved and aggravated into something supernatural. This was undoubtedly the case of all the heathen miracles; and though it may hurt in some measure the general credit of miracles, yet, as experience has plainly shewn, it has not in any degree affected the credit of common history. For example. *Dionysius of Halicarnassus* is esteemed one of the most faithfull and accurate historians of antiquity: we take his word without scruple, and preferably even to the Roman writers, in his account of the civil affairs of *Rome*; yet we laugh at the fictitious miracles which he has interspersed in it. "In the war with the *Latins*," he tells us, "how the gods, *Castor and Pollux*, appeared visibly on white horses, and fought on the side of the *Romans*, who by their assistance gained a complete victory; and that for a perpetual memorial of it, a temple was publicly erected, and a yearly festival, sacrifice, and procession instituted to the honor of those deities." Now tho' no body at this day believes a tittle of the miracle, yet the faith of history is not hurt by it. We admit the battel and the victory, and take the miraculous part to be, what it certainly was, the fiction of the commanders or persons interested, contrived for the sake of some private as well as public benefit, which the nature of the case will easily suggest.

Thus in the narrative also, above mentioned, of the Martyrdom of *St. Polycarp*, the point of history is, that he was condemned to death at *Smyrna*, of which he was Bishop; and there actually burnt at the stake for his profession of the Christian faith. We have no doubt therefore of his Martyrdom, yet may reasonably pause at the miracles which are said to have attended it. The voice pretended to come from heaven, was heard only by a few; and that in a time of such hurry, in which nothing could be heard distinctly. If such a voice therefore had been uttered by any one in the croud, as it was hardly possible to discern whence it came, so those whose zeal and imagination were particularly affected by so moving an occasion, might easily mistake it for miraculous. The flame also is said to have made an arch around his body, and could not burn it; an appearance which might easily happen from the common effects of the wind, or something at least so like it as to afford matter enough to a superstitious fancy to supply the rest. But the circumstance of a *dove flying out of his body when pierced by a sword*, is beyond all belief: or if a dove was really seen to fly out of the wood which was prepared to consume him, it might have been conveyed thither, probably by design, in order to be let loose at a certain moment. As in the funerals of the Roman Emperors, an eagle was always observed to fly out of the funeral pile as soon as it began to blaze, which was supposed to convey the soul of the deceased into heaven; of which, a solemn deposition was constantly made upon oath, in order to the deification of those emperors.

But the case of witchcraft affords the most effectual proof of the truth of what I am advancing. There is not in all history any one miraculous fact so authentically attested as the existence of witches. All Christian nations whatsoever have consented in the belief of them, and provided capital laws against them; in consequence of which, many hundreds of both sexes have suffered a cruel death. In our own country, great numbers have been condemned to die, at different times, after a public trial by the most eminent judges of the kingdom: and in some places, for a perpetual memorial of their diabolical practices, anniversary sermons and solemnities have been piously instituted, and subsist at this day to propagate a detestation of them to all posterity. Now to deny the reality of facts so solemnly attested and so universally believed, seems to give the lie to the sense and experience of all christendom, to the wisest and best of every nation, to public monuments subsisting to our own times: yet the incredibility of the thing prevailed, and was found at last too strong for all this force of human testimony; so that the belief of witches is now utterly extinct, and quietly buried without involving history in it's ruin, or leaving even the least disgrace or censure upon it.

There is another instance also, within our own times, more directly applicable to our present purpose. I mean the pretended miracles of the late Abbé de Paris, which made such a noise in France a few years ago, and are still believed by a great part of that kingdom, or by all perhaps who believe any other miracles of that Church. This Abbé was a zealous *Jansenist*, and warm opposer of that Bull or Constitution of *Pope Clemens* XI., called *Unigenitus*, by which all the doctrines of his sect were expressly condemned. He died in 1725, and was buried in the church-yard of *St. Medard* in *Paris*; whither the great reputation of his sanctity drew many people to visit his tomb, and pay their devotions to him as to a saint: and this concourse gradually increasing, made him soon be considered as a subject proper to revive the credit of that party, now utterly depressed by the power of the Jesuits, supported by the authority of the Court. Within six years therefore after his death, the confident report of miracles, wrought at his tomb, began to alarm not onely the City of Paris, but the whole nation; while infinite crouds were perpetually pressing to the place, and proclaming the benefits received from the saint: nor could all the power of the Government give a check to the rapidity of this superstition, till by inclosing the tomb within a wall, they effectually obstructed all access to it.

This expedient, tho' it put an end to the external worship of the Saint, could not shake the credit of his miracles; distinct accounts of which were carefully drawn up and dispersed among the people, with an attestation of them much more strong and authentic than what has ever been alledged for the miracles of any other age since the days of the Apostles. *Mons. de Montgeron*, a person of eminent rank in *Paris*, published a select number of them in a pompous volume in quarto, which he dedicated to the King, and presented to him in person; being induced to the publication of them, as he declares, by the incontestable evidence of the facts, by which he himself, from a libertin and professed Deist, became a sincere convert to the Christhan faith. But besides the collection of Mr. *de Montgeron*, several other collections were made, containing in the whole above an hundred miracles, which are all published together in three volumes, with their original vouchers, certificates, affidavits, and letters annexed to each of them at full length.

The greatest part of these miracles were employed in the cures of desperate diseases, in their last and deplored state, and after all human remedies had for many years been tried upon them in vain; but the patients no sooner addressed themselves to the tomb of this Saint, than the most inveterate cases, and complications of palsies, apoplexies, and dropsies, and even blindness and lameness, &c., were either instantly cured, or greatly relieved, and within a short time after wholly removed. All which cures were performed in the Churchyard of St. *Medard*, in the open view of the people, and with so general a belief of the finger of God in them, that many *Infidels*, *Debauché's*, *Schismatics*, and *Heretics* are said to have been converted by them to the Catholic faith. And the reality of them is attested by some of the principal physicians and surgeons in France, as well as the clergy of the first dignity, several of whom were eye-witnesses of them, who presented a verbal procès of each to the archbishops, with a petition signed by above twenty *curés* or rectors of the parishes of *Paris*, desiring that they might be authentically registered, and solemnly published to the people, as true miracles.

I have seen an answer to these miracles by a Protestant writer, *Mr. Des Voeux*; who does not deny the facts, but the miraculous nature of them only, which by many reasons he endeavours to render suspected. Yet another writer on the same side, declares that all his reasons are too weak to do them any hurt; and that there is no other way of shaking their credit, than by shewing them to be the works of the Devil. Which he undertakes to prove, in three letters to the said *Mr. Des Voeux*, to be the genuin character of them.

Let our declamers then on the authority of the Fathers, and the faith of history, produce, if they can, any evidence of the primitive miracles, half so strong as what is alledged for the miracles of the *Abbé de Paris*; or if they cannot do it, let them give us a reason why we must receive the one, and reject the other: or if they fail likewise in this, let them be so ingenuous at last as to confess, that we have no other part left, but either to admit them all, or reject them all; for otherwise, they can never be thought to act consistently. And if, from their avowed principles and blind deference to authority, we may guess at their real sentiments in the present case, they will be as little scrupulous about the modern as the ancient miracles of the Church, but patiently admit them all; as being more agreeable to that rule which is prescribed by their primitive guides,—"that the true disciples of Christ, *have nothing more to do with curiosity or inquiry; but when they are once become believers, their sole business is to believe on.*"

Again; the celebrated historian, *Mr. de Vertot*, whose *Revolutions of Rome, of Sweden, and of Por-*

tugal, afford so much entertainment to the public, has written a defence also of a certain miracle, which is imagined to do some honor to the Church and kingdom of France; I mean the miracle of *the sacred vial*, or *sainte Ampoulle*, as it is called, with which their kings are anointed at their coronation.

This vial is said to have been brought from heaven by a dove, for the baptismal unction of *Clovis, the first Christian king of France*; and dropped into the hands of St. *Remigius*, then Bishop of *Rheims*, about the end of the fifth century; where it has been preserved ever since for the purpose of anointing all succeding kings. And it's divine descent is said to be confirmed by this miracle; that *as soon as the coronation is over, the oil in the vial begins to wast and vanish, but is constantly renewed of itself, for the service of each new coronation.*

The *Abbe de Vortot* defends the truth of this miracle by the authority of several witnessess, who lived at the time of *Remigius* or near to it; and of many later writers also, who give testimony to the same, through each succeding age. Yet a learned Professor at *Utrecht*, in a dissertation upon this subject, treats it as a mere forgery, or pious fraud, contrived to support the dignity of the *Kings and Clergy of France*; and ranks it in the same class with the *Palladium of Troy; the Ancilia of old Rome; and the Cross which Constantin pretended to see in the heavens*; and the rest of those political fictions, which we meet with in the histories of all ages.

Now what will our Advocates of the primitive miracles say to this? Will they tell us here, as they have often done on similar occasions, that by rejecting the authority of *Mr. Vertot* and his witnesses in this story, we destroy the faith of all his other stories, and can no longer take his word for any thing, which he has related of *Rome*, or *Sweden*, or *Portugal*? Let them talk at this silly rate as long as they please, men of sense will always know how to distinguish in such cases; how to extract all the instruction, which is offered to them, in one part of his writings; yet guard themselves from all the superstition which is inculcated in the other. They know, that, on subjects of common history, a writer of sense and credit can hardly have any other motive of writing, but to please and instruct, and to illustrate the truth of facts, as far as he was able, by the perspicuity of his stile, and the proper disposition of his materials: but on subjects of a miraculous kind, they know likewise, how forcibly the prejudices of education, a superstitious turn of mind, the interests of a party, or the views of ambition are apt to operate on a defender of those miracles, which the government and religion of his country are engaged to support.

These few instances are sufficient to evince the reasonableness and prudence of suspending our assent to reports of a miraculous kind, tho' attested by an authority, which might safely be trusted in the report of ordinary events. They teach us also how opinions, wholly absurd and contrary to nature, may gain credit and establishment through ages and nations, which, by the force of education, custom, and example, have once contracted a superstitious and credulous turn; till being checked from time to time by the gradual improvements of science, and the successive efforts of reason, inquiring occasionally into the uncertain grounds, and reflecting on the certain mischiefs of them, they have fallen at last into such utter contempt, as to make us wonder, how it was possible for them, ever to have obtained any credit.

But whatever be the uncertainty of ancient history, there is one thing at least which we may certainly learn from it; that human nature has always been the same; agitated by the same appetites and passions, and liable to the same excesses and abuses of them, in all ages and countries of the world; so that our experience of what passes in the present age, will be the best comment on what is delivered to us concerning the past. To apply it then to the case before us: there is hardly a single fact, which I have charged upon the primitive times, but what we still see performed in one or other of the Sects of Christians of our own times. Among some we see *diseases cured, Devils cast out, and all the other miracles* which are said to have been wrought in the primitive Church; among others we see the boasted gifts of *Tertullian's* and *Cyprian's* days; *pretended revelations, prophetic visions, and divine impressions:* now all these modern pretensions we readily ascribe to their true cause; to the artifices and craft of a few, playing upon the credulity, the superstition, and the enthusiasm of the many, for the sake of some private interest: when we read therefore that the same things were performed by the ancients, and for the same ends, of acquiring a superiority of credit, or wealth, or power, over their fellow creatures; how can we possibly hesitate to impute them to the same cause, of fraud and imposture?

In a word; to submit our belief implicitely and indifferently to the mere force of authority in all cases, whether miraculous or natural, without any rule of discerning the credible from the incredible, might support indeed the faith, as it is called, but would certainly destroy the use of all history; by leading us into perpetual errors, and possessing our minds with invincible prejudices, and false notions both of men and things. But to distinguish between things totally different from each other; between miracle and nature; the extraordinary acts of God and the ordinary transactions of man; to suspend our belief of the one, while, on the same testimony, we grant it freely to the other; and to require a different degree of evidence for each, in proportion to the different degrees of their credibility; is so far from hurting the credit of history, or of any thing else which we ought to believe, that it is the onely way to purge history from it's dross, and render it beneficial to us; and by a right use of our reason and judgement, to raise our minds above the low prejudices and childish superstitions of the credulous vulgar.

FINIS.

The Introductory Discourse concludes thus: "The many corruptions which crept into the Church in those very early ages, are a standing proof and admonition to all the later ages, that there is no way of preserving a purity of faith and worship in any Church, but by reviewing them from time to time, and reducing them to the original test and standard of the Holy Scriptures."

And thus Oxford is invited to do justice in other respects to the Church and itself, as well as by having raised at last an elegant testimonial to the memory of those venerable Protestant martyrs —*Ridley*, *Latimer*, and *Cranmer*—who suffered there so long since as 1555 and 6.

CONTENTS.

Chillingworth is particularly noticed at page 40, and St. *Athanasius*, page 112, of this New Edition.

LIST OF THE PRIMITIVE FATHERS,

TAKEN FROM TOMLINE'S THEOLOGY.

Barnabas	Contemporaries of the Apostles.
Clement of Rome	Contemporaries of the Apostles.
Hermas	Contemporaries of the Apostles.
Ignatius	Contemporaries of the Apostles.
Polycarp	Contemporaries of the Apostles.

Papias	116	Alexander of Alexandria	313
Justin Martyr	140	Eusebius	315
Dionysius of Corinth	170	Athanasius	326
Tatian	172	Cyril of Jerusalem	348
Hegesippus	173	Hilary	354
Melito	177	Epiphanius	368
Irenæus	178	Basil	370
Athenagoras	178	Gregory of Nazianzum	370
Miltiades	180	Gregory of Nyssa	370
Theophilus	181	Optatus	370
Clement of Alexandria	194	Ambrose	374
Tertullian	200	Philaster	380
Minutius Felix	210	Jerome	392
Ammonius	220	Theodore of Mopsuestia	394
Origen	230	Ruffin	397
Firmilian	233	Augustine	398
Dionysius of Alexandria	247	Chrysostom	398
Cyprian	248	Sulpitius Severus	401
Novatus, or Novatian	251	Cyril of Alexandria	412
Arnobius	306	Theodoret	423
Lactantius	306	Gennadius	494

Walton & Mitchell, Printers, 24, Wardour-st., Oxford-st.

Lightning Source UK Ltd.
Milton Keynes UK
UKHW021955121219
355294UK00007B/228/P